MW01241548

Easy Article Templates

Article Writing Success Made Easy: Simple Idea-Starters To Create Quality, Unique Content FAST

Version 3.0
Robert Boduch
Copyright © All rights reserved worldwide.
ISBN: 978-0-9811807-5-5

thesuccesstrack@gmail.com
http://bizprofitbuilder.com/

Table of Contents

How To Write Articles Fast: Laying the Foundation for Quick and Easy Content Creation

With this information, you'll be quite capable of writing articles in minutes instead of hours. Sure, you'll need to learn the basics -- but it isn't difficult at all. With practice, you'll write better quality content in less time than ever before.

Articles are a fundamental tool for marketing online. The internet as we know it today is a massive repository of information. A basic search on Google, Bing, or any other search engine will turn up a bounty of articles on any and every conceivable subject. If you can think it, you can pretty much guarantee someone has written about it.

Though there are numerous additional formats for the exchange and dissemination of information online including reports, ebooks, podcasts, video, reviews, forums, webinars and more - **the simple article is the basic foundation. Most everything is a derivative of an idea which could be described in a short article.**

Anyone can learn to write articles quickly and make them pay off handsomely – and every entrepreneur, affiliate marketer, and small business should be using this strategy. Many experienced marketers hire others to write their articles. If you've got the budget, this can be a terrific way to consistently grow your enterprise by continually adding fresh, new content to your site or blog – or use it to attract prospects from far and wide.

The articles I'm talking about are short, punchy and to-the-point. They're mini-lessons that offer valuable, specific information as quickly and directly as possible.

This type of article delivers information fast. It may contain as few as 400 words, though is typically slightly longer -- in the 500-800 word range. Not exactly the kind of article you would submit to a magazine for publishing, but certainly something you can use on your web site to provide helpful content for visitors. But that's not to say that you can't use these strategies to create longer articles too and significantly reduce the two or three hours of work time it typically takes. Just be aware that you'll need to cover much more ground.

If you want to master quick article creation on demand – you've got to focus on cranking out those relatively short but informative pieces.

Every article you compose - even short blog posts - can be valuable tools that work for you and your business around the clock. This is the case as long as you're committed to providing useful information to your readers. This above all else is the key to delivering value and attracting a larger readership and gaining plenty of click-throughs.

Each article can help build your business, regardless of the current size or sales volume of your operation. Articles can work just as effectively for the micro-business as they can for any sizable organization. It's a matter of getting decent content out there and generating plenty of interest.

But any single piece is just one business-building tool. That's why you need to create a large volume of articles over time and for this kind of prolific writing – you'll need some sort of simple writing system.

Your most effective articles could potentially generate thousands of prospects, customers, subscribers, regular visitors, or members. Others will be far less useful as marketing tools. But you just don't know how each individual article will perform until it's out there in the marketplace for all to see.

Volume is one of the secrets. That's why I encourage you to write lots of articles on an ongoing basis. But this can only happen when you become an efficient and productive article writer.

To generate quality content quickly, get organized and focused during whatever time you can find to write. It doesn't have to (nor should it) take hours to write a single piece. With a little practice, you'll find yourself cranking out useful tips and helpful, informative pieces faster than ever. Just keep writing and you'll soon verify the accuracy of what I'm saying here.

Bang those articles out in volume and then let your content do the heavy lifting. Think of each piece you write as a tool for capturing the attention and interest of leads and prospects. That's article marketing 101.

Do it consistently and your business will continue to prosper. Articles are the ultimate lead generating tool, delivering to your web site and your business the kind of people that are an ideal match for your products and services.

Powerful Marketing Magnets Through Useful Content

Article writing is a proven business-building tool. As with any positive action step, the more you do it, the easier it gets. Focus on providing useful content in your articles. Make content creation part of your routine and it will pay off handsomely for you in the long run.

When you post your articles to an online directory and include a compelling resource box with a relevant link back to your site, you will attract interested visitors to your site.

The more of these original articles you post, the higher you ultimately tend to rank in the search engines for those specific terms related to your theme or topic. That's a basic marketing strategy that costs nothing, can be done by anyone, and has the potential to make a significant impact on your business.

All published articles provide you additional opportunities to get the word out about you and your site/business. Each piece helps build credibility and establish expertise in your area of specialty.

The more articles written and submitted related to your specific target market, the more lead-generating seeds you've planted. Spread those seeds regularly and you will reap a bountiful harvest – that's the power of marketing through content. It's an inevitable result, provided you select a decent market niche, share valuable content and target the right keyword terms.

Write those pieces yourself and they cost you nothing but time. That's what makes article writing such a powerful marketing tool for anyone just getting started online. But articles shouldn't be limited to the beginner. Every individual and organization - large and small - should be utilizing articles as part of their business-building strategy. It doesn't matter if they're written internally or outsourced. Articles represent content and original and useful content delivers value in the vast online world.

Studies show that the overwhelming majority of people online are seeking information of some kind. The internet is where most people turn to conduct basic research on products, people and places. Most go directly to a site like Google and enter specific information in the search window – information that summarizes whatever is on their mind. They want something specific and the search engines are quick to serve up multiple choices.

It's the mission of those search engines is to deliver the most relevant information requested by users. Since people want on-target, up-to-date information from the most recent and qualified articles written, that's what usually gets delivered. This means that relevant information of value gets preferential treatment over anything else and articles fill the need and play the role perfectly. If you want more search engine love - write more quality articles because they help fulfill the requests of online users. And the more effective a particular search engine is at matching a request with specific information, the more its users will return again and again to the same search engine because it delivers reliably.

The more articles you upload to your own site, the more value you provide to visitors in terms of content and the more your site becomes an asset of increasing value. Submit more relevant, one-of-a-kind articles and chances are your search engine positioning will improve as your site grows in authority in your particular area of specialty.

If you want to build your reputation as an expert in a niche, add more content to your site on a regular basis. If you want you create a resource-based niche site and generate revenue from an advertising program such as Google's Adsense, you'll fare far better with hundreds - or thousands - of articles than you would with just a few. Quantity and quality count in building authority and trust.

Successful blogging works the same way.

Each post made to a blog is essentially a short article. Specialize in a niche topic or your favourite area of expertise and you'll gradually build your web-based asset. Provide helpful and relevant information and you'll magnetically draw more readers, members, subscribers, customers, reviewers, and fans who share the same interests.

Article marketing is here to stay because a well-written article adds value to both the online business it represents and the community at large. It's useful material. Whatever the format or application, your content should always serve your target audience. Choose your market and then let your articles provide detailed information of benefit to this specific group of people.

Writing Articles is an Investment in Time or Money

Writing is an investment. You either invest time or money – there's no getting away from making an investment of some sort.

If it were possible to push a button and instantly and automatically have a 100%-original and quality article created for you, then maybe you could sit back in your lounge chair sipping a cocktail at the beach and have your business continue to grow on autopilot. But the next best thing is to discover a way to create fresh, unique, high-value written content in a flash.

Of course, you'd still have to buy the software, if in fact it were available. But in the absence of such a miraculous tool for article creation, the only other choices are to roll up your sleeves and get down to it - or hire someone else to write for you. But writing an article need not be a difficult task that takes forever. If you've got a few minutes – I'll show you how to get it done efficiently.

You can then use this written content numerous ways – on your site or elsewhere – to draw targeted traffic your way. You could even convert your content to audio or video materials and exponentially expand your marketing firepower.

I suspect that for most people, writing an article seems like a chore. That's why they don't even consider it, preferring instead to search endlessly for some "secret formula" that will give them what they want. For those who decide to go for it, the majority spend as little time as possible, exerting only minimal energy in the process of writing articles. You can probably guess that results are less than positive with this kind of approach.

If you're serious about generating business online, you need to share information regularly. You can do so in the form of articles, short reports, ebooks, podcasts, or videos as part of your overall content marketing strategy.

The easiest way to begin is with articles. If you write them yourself, it's a simple, cost-free way to get started.

Informative articles serve as helpful resources – assets that deliver true value to those seeking out the specific information you share. A consistent program of creating and publishing original articles related to your area of specialty can only help you in the long run.

But it need not take you a whole afternoon to piece together a single article. In fact, it shouldn't take you an hour, or even thirty minutes to produce one article. Sure, you won't hit your optimum stride right off the bat - nobody does. It will probably take you longer in the beginning, but that's the way it is with learning any new skill. Then as you gain experience and knowledge, your abilities improve and your writing speed skyrockets.

I'm going to show you what I believe is the quickest way possible to create quality articles that are completely unique in every way. This method does not involve PLR, (Private Label Rights) products, content scraping, or taking (stealing) other people's content and rewriting it. I'm talking about 100%-original content that is yours and yours alone.

Soon you will be capable of cranking out articles faster than you ever imagined. It will transform your content-creation productivity. You'll be able to literally write some articles in mere minutes. Others may take a bit longer, but you'll still be producing your own content at an accelerated pace.

I urge you to go through this process and begin writing at least some of your own articles. Incorporate these simple techniques into your strategy and you'll notice an improvement in writing speed almost immediately.

Later, you can continue to write articles yourself, or have someone else write them for you. Numerous outsourcing options exist – and at various price points. As your budget allows, you can combine outsourced content with articles you've personally written to dramatically expand your content and marketing clout.

A third option is to outsource all article creation. Once you've found writers who can consistently deliver quality, original work at a price that's reasonable and affordable, this could prove to be a terrific investment in your business. I know of one online marketer who claims to regularly invest about $4,000 every month on fresh articles written by ghostwriters. When your business is in a position to do so, that may be something you want to consider too. Then again, when you see for yourself how easy it is to write articles lightning-fast, you may reconsider, or assign the task internally, or pass it off to a virtual assistant.

Either way, if you're new to content creation, it's best to start on a solid footing and reserve any available cash. This usually means writing your own articles.

Article Writing: A Proven Way To Make Money Online

Writing articles is easy once you find your groove. Make it part of your routine. As you do, you'll turn into a writing machine and the words will flow, practically on autopilot. For maximum efficiency, you need to learn a proven system or develop your own.

Adapt whatever methods work best for you and you'll consistently convert small windows of opportunity into highly-productive content generation sessions.

Write and submit more quality articles and you can quickly become a dominant player in virtually any market or industry. That's the power of the written word - delivered with authority - and it's available to anyone.

Find out what your market wants to know – that's step number one. Then, deliver it in short, informative segments. An article is the ideal vehicle for serving today's busy information consumers perfectly. In about one page of content, you can deliver solid, informative and actionable material.

Apply these concepts daily and you'll consistently build a stronger online presence and draw more traffic too. What you'll also find is this: those visitors you attract from your articles are highly-targeted. This means they're pre-qualified prospects for your products and/or services.

Articles placed in directories gives you a chance to strut your stuff and show what you know to people who've never heard of you and who may not have found your site or blog any other way.

Let's face it: any task that is seemingly difficult, time-consuming, or boring is something most of us will avoid at all costs. We're simply wired that way. If it seems like it's going to be a pain in the neck to do, we tend to run in the opposite direction.

But perception is everything. If you change what a difficult task means to you, it quickly loses it power and control and becomes much less daunting.

Writing content is a lot like having one of those deep conversations with a good friend. Imagine a friend asking you a probing question about one of your passions. Could you give a quality response in three to seven minutes? Of course you could. Oh and your detailed response is essentially an article.

That's really all it takes when you know your subject well and can articulate it clearly sand passionately.

Taking the attitude that you can master article writing is something that will get you started in the right direction. Having practical, time-saving information and tools to make article writing a snap, will help make regular writing part of your day or week.

Armed with the right knowledge, writing simple articles is no longer something you'll automatically avoid. After you've used this effective system and begin to see positive results, you'll understand the value in continuing at the same pace, or expanding your efforts on a broader scale.

Make article writing as easy and efficient as possible. Get an idea, quickly generate a short outline and then expand on your idea in sentences and paragraphs. You'll vastly improve your production - and boost your traffic, leads, subscribers, customers, cash flow, and profits too in the process.

A Quick and Easy Way To Gain Expertise on Any Subject

The process of writing an individual article should be a simple task. For maximum effect, it's best to include regular articles as part of your ongoing marketing procedures, so you build awareness and recognition in your marketplace over time.

What I want you to understand is that "writing" is only a part of the process of article creation. Sure, it's the part that's the most fun. But the key to lightning-fast article production lies in the preparation. The writing stage is where you share your thoughts in sentences. But for high-output article writing, much of the "work" is taken care of in the preliminary steps.

It's important to know your topic - that should be obvious. But it's surprising how many times inexperienced writers try to wing it. Think about the kind of reader or prospect you want to attract to your web site or business. Then give these folks the kind of information that will draw their attention because of its value and usefulness.

Faking it won't get you very far. You're better off in the long run to gain a sound understanding of your overall niche and subject matter before attempting to come off as an expert. Thankfully this can be accomplished fairly quickly by speed reading the top 7-12 books, manuals, or courses on your subject. You may not be an established expert. But you'll be astonished at how much more you know about your subject than most – and you'll gain this knowledge in short order by following this approach.

Pay particular attention to the current voices of authority in your field. Who are the experts in the niche that people are listening to the most? Who are the recognized authorities, both online and offline? Join groups and forums using a pseudonym and seek out the top names and best resources available to really understand your subject in a hurry. You want to learn from the best so your online article writing will make an impact on your audience.

As an example, if you were to ask me for the top experts in the field of writing advertising copy, I would suggest these five as being at the very top of the list: Gary Bencivenga,

Clayton Makepeace, John Carlton, Gary Halbert and Dan Kennedy. Of course there are dozens more too. But I'm quite confident that if you studied just a few of the resources offered by these "top dogs" and you were passionate about learning the craft, you would gain a serious background in copy writing much faster than muddling through the subject any other way.

If you fail to gain a sufficient background in your area before launching your article writing machine, you'll defeat the purpose. You don't have to reach world-class status before sharing what you've learned. But you should do your homework and gain the necessary background knowledge and some experience before spreading the word about what you know.

Your objective is to produce many articles over the months and years ahead and to get them working for you. But job one is to take the preliminary step of immersing yourself in your subject of interest. Do this and you'll have a foundational knowledge base that can help you create hundreds of unique pieces of content.

A background in your subject gives you a solid footing. Without adequate understanding on your part, any new information will seem foreign to you. You won't have a good grasp of it and therefore, cannot do an adequate job of explaining the finer details to your audience.

With this foundation in place, you can then get going on your article production. Remember: the intention here is to help you produce quality articles quickly and easily. So everything about your methods or system should be designed to facilitate this process.

Treat online article writing as an essential part of your business. It's free marketing and exposure. All it takes is time and a desire to communicate helpful ideas with your audience.

Every minute spent effectively on one aspect of article writing is a minute invested in building your online presence and growing your business. Consistent, daily action yields the best results. If you continue to add new articles regularly, you will see a substantial return for what amounts to a comparatively small effort each day. What makes your time investment extra valuable is that you will continue to reap the compounding rewards as you continue to publish more articles.

3 Simple Secrets To Writing Articles For Money

Writing articles and making them pay off is often a numbers game. You've got to produce a steady stream of articles to maximize the return on your time investment. To accomplish this, you need a simple and straightforward approach to writing.

Articles attract genuine customers and that's the best kind of traffic you can get. This applies whether you're selling your own products, earning advertising revenues from a content site, or generating affiliate commissions by promoting other people's products.

Keep it simple and you're more inclined to put forth those daily actions because you'll be able to shift into article writing gear without first stopping to think about it. Simple is better. Keep this in mind and don't overcomplicate the process.

The easiest method I've found is to have an ongoing large list of potential article topics. With much to choose from – you're ready to roll at a moment's notice.

When you're in a creative mindset, review your list and generate as many additional potential article topics as you can comfortably map out in a single session. With this simple framework in hand, crafting a few meaningful paragraphs is a breeze. This is a big part of being able to write articles consistently - even when other issues are weighing heavily on your mind.

If it seems to be too much work, most people will avoid it. But having a basic outline is the secret to making content writing super-easy and lightning-quick.

Don't bite off more than you can chew. It's best to start small with three to five articles at a time and expand as you get comfortable using this method of writing.

Take your articles one at a time and flesh out the content. I'll show you several ways to do this a little later. Having a rough idea of what you want to communicate gives you substance – it's something concrete to work with. Just a few details about each article in the form of single words, symbols, or point-form essentials, and you have a plan of the article in no time. Now you're ready to write.

Allow extra time for editing, polishing and publishing to your site or an article directory. When posting to directories, it's important to have several resource boxes ready so you can simply plug them into any article you want and modify to suit. With a collection of resources to draw from, it's only a matter of connecting the dots, as you'll see when you start using the resources provided at the back of the book.

There are three keys to achieving maximum article productivity in minimum time. They are:

1. Use templates to automate article writing wherever possible
2. Create a simple map, framework, or outline for each article
3. Write as fast as you can for a set time period only

We will explore each of these keys and others as well. Having the capability to turn out article after article on demand is the underlying concept of efficient and profitable article writing. But you also need to deliver helpful information, whether a particular piece is destined for a directory or your own site.

Quality, unique content clearly communicated to a targeted prospect is the essence of a powerful and effective article that can pay off for everybody.

Include frequently searched for keywords and you help shape your articles to fit what those in your niche market are seeking. This is somewhat important because these are the exact words prospects use when searching for information on the topic. By speaking their language, you're building a bridge of trust and comfort for the people you want to reach. Just don't go crazy with keywords and use them sparingly. Focus instead on producing useful information and building your asset base.

The key to writing articles for maximum money is to go deep – and that means using "long-tail" keyword terms. Long tails are multiple-word terms - typically three to five words in length, but potentially with as many as ten words. These longer keyword terms have far less competition, so it's generally easier to rank higher for those terms and they tend to attract a better quality of prospect too.

Proven Format Makes It as Easy as Paint-By-Numbers

When it comes to actually writing those articles, the natural reaction of many beginners is to put it off until later. All the advantages of publishing articles - increased traffic, subscribers and instant sales - sound good on the surface. But the overriding fear most people have is that writing is just plain hard work. It's easier to shy away from the toil. But let's break down those perceived barriers once and for all so you begin to benefit on a grander scale.

Let's assume you had a goal of writing 100 articles to promote a single product. Online articles are typically about 300-800 words in length, or about 1-2 pages of text each. If you look at the whole project of crafting 100 articles, in some ways, it's a lot like writing a 100-page+ book.

But if you were to take just one page and focus on that part of the puzzle, writing a solid page of content would become a more manageable task.

Now let's take it one step further. Instead of pondering the article in its entirety, look at the various elements and handle those one at a time.

Anatomy of an Article

When you break it down to its essence, you'll notice that there are just five component pieces to most articles. These include...

- Title or Headline
- Opening or Lead Paragraphs
- Content or Body Copy of the Article
- Conclusion or Summary
- Resource Box (to be used when posting to article directories, writing for other ezines, or guest-blogging)

Every article begins with a title, followed by the lead paragraph. The title plays the same role the headline does in advertising. Its main purpose is to attract interest and compel readers to read on. Next, the content paragraphs provide the essential information. Then the conclusion wraps it up.

It all needs to flow smoothly as one, rather than a bunch of separate pieces stuck together. But if you have a good idea of what you want to say in each section, it's far easier to write that article in one fell swoop. If you're struggling, try breaking the article down into pieces. This format of content creation simplifies the process.

The final piece of the puzzle is the resource box. It's designed to attract readers to click on the link within and send them to a designated page on your site. Ultimately, that's the action you want to encourage your readers to take.

Create your resource box in advance. Better yet, write several different ones, or use the resource box idea triggers found here for inspiration. That's the easiest way to get started and you won't get hung up at the finish line. Instead, you'll be able to use your content straight away.

Capture Your Audience with a Compelling Title

Nothing is more important to the success of your articles than the titles you select.

Titles act as headlines to announce your content to targeted audiences. It's the title that tells your potential reader what you've got to offer. Instantaneously, a decision is made as to whether or not it's of enough interest to be worth the reader's time.

You'll want to get your keyword into the title and as close to the front as possible. That's one step towards getting more favourable attention from the search engines. At the same time, you'll be serving up the exact keyword terms searchers seek. When they stumble upon your article, they're more likely to be pulled inside. Of all the article writing tips you find, nothing has the same, double whammy impact as a carefully-crafted title. Titles play a key role.

Write your article title in a similar fashion to a headline. Consider the title like a flagman on the side of the road directing traffic around a detour. Your title has to grab readers by the eyeballs and compel them to come inside and read on - in order to gain the benefit of your entire message.

The title is the one thing potential prospects see before making a split-second decision to stick around or to sail right on by. If your title elicits anything but a "tell me more" thought in the reader's mind, you can be sure that she won't waste another conscious second on it and will move onto the next available option.

Target your prospect in the title and you will momentarily at least, capture the exact audience you seek. When you identify the specific reader your article was written for in the title, you instantly sound the alarm for every member of this particular group and you can be certain these people will pay attention to your online article. By doing so you call attention to your customized topic, written for a specific group of people. Few others would even be interested. But you can bet the huge majority who fit the profile of your target audience will latch onto your information the way a dog latches onto a bone.

Capture the essence of what your article delivers to the target audience and trumpet that in your title.

Think from your reader's perspective and announce what you article covers in an interesting, compelling and benefit-oriented way. Benefits convey value and the juicier and more intriguing the promised benefit, the more alluring the article.

You want your audience to figuratively salivate after reading the title, so more of them will click through to your article. If your title doesn't trigger that instant interest mechanism inside, readers will flee. When that happens you've missed the boat on what was possibly your only opportunity to draw potential buyers inside.

Make it more advantageous to go ahead and read your article, rather than skip it. That's all you can ask of any title, really.

When you stop and think about it, you soon realize that the only tool you have at your disposal for capturing an audience is the title. That's why you need to give it all you've got. Your task in title writing is to attract maximum readership. The more readers you pull in, the larger your pool of potential cash-spending customers.

How To Pull Prospects In With Your Opening Paragraph

One sure-fire article writing tip that can pay huge dividends is to have your first sentence and paragraph pick up where your article title left off.

This makes sense because you've already aroused interest with a strong title that induced further involvement. Now it's up to the content you provide to fulfill on the promise of your title. If you want to use articles and build your business, you've got to keep readers on the line.

But you need to be quick off the mark. No dilly-dallying, or you'll lose them in a flash.

Think about what it was that got your reader to go beyond the title in the first place. This is a key to having the piece pay off for you. It could have been an exact keyword phrase, or the promise of an irresistible, on-target benefit.

Something about your title, or some element of it compelled the reader to click the link and continue reading in order to get the whole story. Staying on the same track gives you the best odds of having readers continue along the path already started.

Your opening paragraph is somewhat of a test. Busy online readers scurry about and have zero tolerance for anything that could possibly take them off their course. So be sure to give your readers what they came for, beginning with the opening paragraph.

Continuing with the theme of your title sends a signal to online readers that they are in fact exactly where they should be. That's a sound article writing strategy that will serve you well. It's the reinforcement of your big promise.

But now that they've arrived at the place you want them to be, they're once again looking for a reason to leave.

Why?

Because what often happens with early search results is they fail to hit the mark for specific, targeted information. It's not uncommon to not find what you want from the first few results a search engine spits out. In effect, each step on the search path is a stepping stone to more searching.

So, despite the power of your title, most incoming traffic is looking for a reason to flee. They don't expect to find what they want, so the slightest indication of a fading interest and they're out of there. So when you publish articles online and you hit that sweet spot, readers are quite naturally pulled towards your site and any other offerings you might have.

Every paragraph and every sentence you write needs to pull readers towards the next, like metal shavings to a magnet. It's got to give them a reason to read on. And the paragraph you open your articles with is the most crucial test of all, since it's likely their first encounter with your content. Keep this simple writing insight in your back-pocket whenever you set out to craft your articles.

Whatever it was that got the reader to this point should now be emphasized. Use the promise of the title like gasoline on fire. It's the title that kindled interest. Now turn that interest up a notch by continuing in the same direction. It's a reliable way to instantly strengthen your relationship with your reader and ensure your article draws an audience.

When you underscore the big benefit within the opening paragraph, you confirm to the reader why she's there. It's reassurance. You've won her over for the time being, but her finger is forever on the trigger and any dip in interest level and off she goes.

Openings set the tone. It's always best to make your articles easy and inviting. If it looks like a chore to get through your content – it's easy to pass it up and move on.

Short sentences and paragraphs make for faster reading. If it looks too daunting to read, most people won't bother, even when they're seemingly interested in the topic. So break up your text into small bite-size pieces.

Think of your first paragraph as a sip from a spoon, rather than a giant mouthful that's difficult to chew. Set the stage for the content that follows. Build on the interest that's already stirred. When you do that, you give your article writing power. It's the best opportunity to maximize the value of each piece you write from this point onward.

How To Deliver The Content Readers Want

When it comes to writing articles that make a splash, the one constant is solid content. This generally means at least four or five paragraphs (and often more) containing important details or tips on your topic. Good content adds value to the vast online library and it helps build your brand as it boosts the trust others have in you.

Your title acted as the tag to capture interest. Next, the opening framed the subject to prepare the reader for the angle you chose to take. Now it's time to deliver content and this is where the rubber meets the road. It's at this point that you've got to supply substance in the form of tips, techniques, methods, shortcuts, lessons - or insights gained through research, or experience.

Just remember to keep it simple. You want to serve quality, original content every time and you need to do so with clarity and precision.

You're not writing a book, special report, or even a magazine article for that matter. It's a short informational piece – a to-the-point chunk of content made for immediate online consumption only. Wherever you plan to publish, remember to keep your article short and purposeful. And make it easy to understand and act upon.

You don't need 2500 words to deliver quality information. Not 1500 or 1000 words either. In fact, did you know that you could write as little as 350-450 words and still have your article accepted at many article directories online? It's true. 400 - 500 words and you're in - in most cases. That's generally the new minimum standard, though it doesn't give you a whole lot of space to share your gems – so you could certainly write longer articles if you want to.

Chances are many of your articles will be somewhat longer to fit in crucial details. And you may want to include the odd monster article in your overall repertoire. That's never a bad idea - as long as you provide good content and value. But it's noticeably easier to get started with multiple, short articles – and that's what we're focusing on here.

Since each article you write and post online is another marketing tool in your arsenal capable of drawing thousands of potential customers, it makes sense to place many rather than a few. So if you're sitting on a 1500-word creation, you might be better off dividing it up into two, or maybe even three separate articles.

You'll be giving readers your information in smaller, bite-size pieces, making for easier consumption. And you'll multiply your inbound links and the number of promotional "prospect magnets" you will have working for you.

How To Write Faster Articles and Still Generate Quality, Unique Content Every Time

Here's an easy way to create the foundation of a dynamite article in a matter of seconds. It's something that anyone can do. All you have to do to quickly map out the content of your article almost instantly is this: *learn to think in 3's.*

With every proposed article topic, break it down into three key points.

Take the topic and quickly think of 3 words associated to it. It might be as simple as outlining the 3 steps to accomplishing a particular task… or 3 mistakes people make when attempting something specific.

It's a quick and easy process. Jump right in and you'll write faster articles with greater ease.

Another way to use the concept of "thinking in 3's" is to list the first three points that come to mind when you think about the topic of your article. You might choose to focus on related "power" words, ideas, concepts, secrets, tactics, or methods related to your topic. Thinking in 3's makes creating quality, original content much less daunting. In a matter of seconds, you've generated acceptable article fodder. Then all you need to do is shape it into sentences and paragraphs. If you want a proven, quick article technique - this is it.

All you have to do is break any "how to" information down into 3 basic steps – that's it. What this approach gives you is an easy way to meet the minimum content requirements for your article to be published.

With three points clearly identified, it's easy to write 1 paragraph on each. Add an introduction and a conclusion and you quickly have a five-paragraph piece. In many cases, that's all you need to draft an article. And the best part about this system is that it need not take more than a few minutes of writing time whenever you want to craft a brand new article.

Numbered lists or bullet points are popular among both article writers and readers. In fact articles with titles like "The Top 7 Ways To Help Your Child Get Better Grades" or "5 Inside Secrets of Work-At-Home Moms" would probably command plenty of attention within their respective niches.

From the writer's perspective, crafting this type of article is quick and painless. All you do is compile a simple list. Yes, your list could be longer than 3 items… but it need not be for most purposes. "3 Ways to…" "3 Secrets of…" or "3 Top Tips for…" could each be converted into a winning article for almost any niche. But a list of less than three items isn't really a list. If you haven't got at least three items to cover, simply choose a different format. I'll show you several ways to generate three points quickly in another section.

You don't have to tell the whole story in your article. Provide quality and unique content, yes. But never give away the farm in the process. You want to get the best prospects to your web site or inside your store.

Consider each article to be a means to an end. It's a necessary step to get prospects to your site fast so they can sign up for your newsletter, buy your product, or join your membership. Your article acts as a qualifier by luring interested leads and prospects inside for a reading. But it's the perceived value of your content that determines where they go from there.

Remember to stick to the basics. Don't over-complicate things. Each article is a brief discussion on an interesting and specific topic. So all you really need are three supporting points and you've got it covered. Give readers a tasty sample and lead them to wherever it is they can get more.

Describe each point in a few sentences and soon you've got a paragraph. You can always expand on your content if you choose and at times you may find it desirable to do so -

even necessary. But flesh out your basic content first and you'll find it a simple task to pull together another article.

Decide if what you have is enough, or if you need to add more. But only add content after you've covered the basics with three main points explained in a few easy to write paragraphs. This will help you write faster articles and it's my sincere hope that you put this information to the test. Adapt it to suit your purposes. Modify this simple system so it fits like a glove. Then send an email and tell me about your results.

Sum It All Up in Your Conclusion

Among the final pieces of the puzzle to write is the article conclusion.

One way to tackle the conclusion is to simply wrap up your lesson or information sharing session with a concise summary. Summarize what you've just covered in an expedient way. Just be sure that it's also a little different from your introduction. In other words... don't copy and paste what you said in your opening as a preview of the content. Instead, quickly recap the key points, or remind readers of the value of the information.

Another approach is to let readers know in no uncertain terms what the application of your material can do for them in their lives. This is important as gives your reader a rousing send-off where they can then go and optimize the benefits of your information while you get them to – or keep them on your site.

Reading something new can open eyes and add to one's accumulated storehouse of knowledge. The more value your reader gets from your article, the more they'll appreciate you and the more likely they are to ultimately become a paying customer for your products or services. But the key to real value is to turn any gained knowledge into actual results.

Encourage the application of the information you've just shared. Suggest a few quick and easy ways to put what they've just learned to good use. In other words, nudge readers a bit so they gain something more from your article by suggesting steps they can take to apply their new knowledge to give it substance and instant "use value". Use these article writing basics and you'll be off and running and soon outpacing the competition.

Real learning only comes through action, so it's best to leave your reader with specific directions as to what to do next. This is where your resource box comes into play for published off-site articles. Clicking the link in your resource box is the ultimate action step and hence, the ultimate conclusion. Getting the click is something you'll want to encourage in every article you write.

A Resource Box That Gets Action: The Key To Making The Most of Your Written Articles

If the title is the single most important component of written articles, what's the second most important part? For lead-generating articles, it's got to be the resource box.

When you create a resource box that gets action, your article writing will pay off in spades.

Your resource box is a short, action-oriented paragraph at the end of an article. It's your invitation to further action on the part of the reader. Without a compelling title, your article doesn't stand a chance of attracting many readers. But without a powerfully inviting resource box, your efforts won't do you much good from a marketing perspective.

Truth is… a killer title and awesome article can bring in boatloads of prospects to your article, wherever it happens to show on the web. But you want them to go further and click on the link at the bottom to bring those people to your offers.

In reality, those who don't click through are of little value to you. They snagged your information and then fled. There's not much in it for you when your prospects leave you. That's why you must do everything in your power to get them to click on that link in your resource box. It's the ultimate action step you want the readers of your article to engage in.

First you attracted the eyeballs of interested prospects. Next, you delivered stellar information of interest to your niche market. Now you've got to make it pay and the only way you can do that is to get more clicks. So you've got to pull out all the stops.

Think of your article as an appealing appetizer. Then, tempt the palette for more. Next, you should offer the BIG

PAYOFF - the full course meal - in your resource box. This is essentially what connects you with your reader and it's a crucial step in gaining value from your article writing work.

Provide an invitation for readers to get more of what they just got. Use the resource box to attract interested prospects to your business by offering something that further satisfies their desire.

Offer a collection of additional, written articles, a free report or ebook, or a downloadable audio or video that is the ideal match to the desires of the market.

Find something these folks would be willing to walk uphill to get and then give them the means to it with a simple link to your site. All they need to do to satisfy their cravings is to click this link and they're off to the races. At the same time, you're filling your funnel with fresh new leads and customers – exactly the kind of people you want to build a relationship with over time.

Every resource box provided represents another gateway to your site and the link is the big payoff point for you. When readers click your link, they're whisked off to your site. That's the first step in the process. Before you can get anyone into your marketing funnel, you first need to lure targeted prospects to visit the page you're directing them towards.

Consider the "click" as a vehicle to the ultimate destination for targeted visitors. You want to create a resource box that gets action - and lots of it. It's your site you're sending prospects to -- or more specifically – a particular page on your web site (like a squeeze page where you give them the opportunity to subscribe) where you can begin the relationship, or initiate some form of revenue generation. Up to this point, all the information you've shared with your prospect has been provided free of charge. Get them to your site and you have the potential to earn actual cash – now and in the future.

Give quality information within your article and then follow that up with a compelling message in the resource box. Do this and you've got a one-two punch that will pull genuine, qualified prospects to your online location.

Think of your written article as a starting point. It's where your target market first discovers the kind of information you deliver. The article is an introduction or entry point, connecting a pool of potential customers to you. Your article is the first link in the chain of what could ultimately lead to a lifetime customer who contributes massive value to your business over the years.

But nothing much happens until you have an offer at the bottom that gets action. You need this component for all your outside articles to step up and do its thing. You've got to get the click to gain any value. It's the natural next step and the real conclusion of each lead-generating piece of content. Make a strong appeal to the kind of person you want to bring in.

SEO Article Writer Secrets - Keyword Terms Help You Several Ways

Keywords play an important role in any article marketing strategy - just ask any SEO article writer. Using the actual keyword terms your market actively searches for helps make your article a good match to the search query. Since it's the intention of the search engines to serve up what its users want, keyword-targeted content makes it easier for your articles to be found.

Keyword use in articles is basic SEO (Search Engine Optimization) at work. Proper use of a particular keyword term within your page of content gets noticed when the search engine crawlers visit a site.

Keyword targeting benefits you whether you've posted to a directory or your own site. When you feature an exact phrase or keyword term, you make it easier for the search engines to find you and provide searches with the relevancy they're looking for. But it's better to draw prospects to your site directly, if you're going to go after keywords.

Most importantly, you want your articles to appeal to a human audience. That's why I prefer to go easy on keyword placement. An article that's stuffed with keywords may earn you recognition from the search robots, but not in a good way. Keyword stuffing is akin to spamming and your article and site will get penalized for it. Blatant overuse of specific terms also has a negative effect on the people you most want to impact – the prospects for your offer.

SEO article writers understand the value of keywords and the importance if using these terms sparingly. You need keywords. But if you use them excessively, you're shooting yourself in the foot.

Use your keyword term once in the title. Repeat the same keyword term once in your lead paragraph. Sprinkle it into your body copy once or twice more and add other variations of the keyword phrase into the mix. You can find the most searched related words by using Google's free keyword tool.

Make it sound as natural as possible – that's important. Write for your readers – not the search engine robots. Keywords need to blend in rather than stand out. Finally, use your same keyword term as a live link in your resource box. That should give you the benefit of keyword utilization for the engines - without turning off readers. There you have it - SEO article writing in a nutshell.

There's no question that utilizing keywords appropriately in your articles can give you greater visibility and more traffic. But don't make it so important that you never get started writing articles because you can't decide which keyword term to begin with.

Fact is… you don't absolutely have to use keywords to begin benefiting from your article writing endeavours. Simply begin sharing useful information. I've known other marketers who only focused on sharing their expertise in the articles they crafted – and these guys have done very well. They didn't worry about keywords, at least not in the beginning. I've used this same approach on occasion too. It can help you get started writing today.

If there's a sizable audience for your topic and your title pulls them in, uploading your non-optimized articles can still result in valuable traffic. But at some point, you'll probably want to incorporate as many actively searched niche market keyword terms as you can into your articles to leverage your writing efforts to the maximum degree.

The value of keywords is that they tell you exactly what your market is searching for. A study of the relevant keywords reveals how a niche market collectively thinks. Tapping into the precise combination of words that people enter into the search field, gives you powerful and precise language to work into your article topics. Doing so is something every skilled SEO article writer does. It effectively means you'll be speaking the same language as the people seeking the information that you provide in your articles.

Keyword research tells you what's on the mind of the people in the marketplace and what sub-topics you should address in your articles.

Get Off To a Great Start by Building a Large Keyword List

If you want to get serious about article marketing, you need to get serious about keywords by building a large keyword list. You can choose from a variety of tools to help - ranging from free to several hundred dollars, or perhaps more. It doesn't really matter which keyword tool you choose as long as you're able to compile a substantial keyword list related to your target market.

Build a massive list of the precise terms people in your market use to seek out related information. Every conceivable keyword combination that's searched at all has the potential to bring customers to you.

Start with the obvious terms that come to mind. Add as many to your list as possible. Then delve deeper into more specific long-tail keyword terms.

Imagine it this way:

First, picture a large tree. Your general topic, usually one or two words, is like the trunk of the tree. Let's use "dog training" as our topic example, so the trunk is represented by the root keyword "dog training".

Each major branch leading from the tree trunk represents a slightly more refined search term. (Example: "puppy dog training")

The smaller branches coming off each main branch are even more specific. These are the long-tail keyword terms you're seeking (remember: these terms are often 4 or 5 words in length and could be as long as 10). (Example: "Labrador puppy dog training in Los Angeles")

Focus on long-tail keyword terms for your content. That's the best way to get started in any niche and it's where building a large keyword list comes in handy. But most new article marketers go for the big numbers, choosing the main market subjects and root keywords instead as their launching point. The problem with this common strategy is that the competition is huge.

To get the best results from your keyword efforts in the shortest possible time, start at the other end of the scale – with some terms that are searched for, but in much lower numbers. This is a proven method to deliver traffic to your site, without being buried by the competition.

Let the big guys duke it out for those giant keywords as you go about building your article empire. Go for a whole bunch of terms for which there is very little competition. This gets you listed on the front page in searches using those specific, long-tail keyword phrases. But get enough of these pages working for you and you'll automatically increase your rankings for the coveted root keywords too as you go about building your own authority site. That's article marketing intelligence that most of us can use to our advantage.

The narrower the search term, the higher the quality of visitor you tend to attract from it. Someone who enters "book on delivering quality training sessions" is probably ready to buy once they find it. Someone else in the same broad market that enters "training ideas" as their search term of choice probably isn't as strong a prospect for the same product - at least not yet.

Starting with general terms gives you lots of opportunities to explore. Each major topic can be further refined into multiple variations of keyword terms.

Growing a large keyword list should be a priority. The more keywords you can collect, the more opportunities you'll have to utilize them in your articles. When you've gathered what you can from your keyword tool of choice, examine your list and do some creative brainstorming of your own. Often this can lead you to another family of related keywords that can prove quite lucrative.

Expand Your List of Keywords and Make More Money

Don't just count on those results your keyword tool of choice generates. Most people do that. If you want to make more money from articles it's best to go beyond the obvious. When you do this, you'll find some true gems that you'll want to use as part of your article strategy.

One way to begin expanding your long-tail keyword list is to use the idea-starters and title triggers provided to come up with a whole series of new possibilities.

Another technique is to start with something specific about your product – like its name or a variation of it. Then add to it to turn it into a term that's likely to be searched for by somebody.

Yet another proven technique is to begin with "buyer keywords" and then expand those terms into variations that might be searched for. Enter any keyword term on Google and frame it with quotation marks and you'll see how many other web sites are listed for that particular term.

Here are some buyer keywords to get you started:

Price or Prices
Bonus or Bonuses
Best
Best Buy
Buy or Buying
Purchase
Top
Top Rated
Review or Reviews
Closeout
Markdowns
Discount
Cheap or Cheaper
Rebate
Ultimate
Deal
For Less
Save Money
Download

The same technique can be applied to those with a pressing
need to find answers and solutions. These terms also tend
to draw in a higher percentage of qualified prospects and
buyers.

Here are some "desperate buyer" terms you may want to
use as triggers for additional long-tail keyword terms:

Improve
Fix
Improve
Beat
Overcome
Better
Faster
Sooner

Cheaper
Help
Advice
Guide
Guidance
How To
Quick Fix
Solve
Resolve
Problems
Solutions
Questions
Answers
FAQ or Frequently Asked Questions
Pros and Cons
Articles
Report
Book
Home Study
Course
Ebook
Video
Tutorial
Online Tutorial
MP3
Instructions
Directions
Support
Get
Get Better
DIY or Do It Yourself

Every possible keyword combo can bring you traffic, so consider as many unique variations as you can.

The suggestion tool built into Google can help you gain additional suggestions for keywords. It's a feature designed to make searching both faster and easier. Enter a term into the search box and Google guesses at what you're looking for and instantly offers suggestions in real time that are popular. So for example, if you type "apple" - you might see alternate terms like "apple pie" or "Apple iPad." What these suggestions allow you to do is to further build your keyword list in the predetermined direction you wish to go.

Here's what happens behind the scenes. To supply those recommendations Google spits out instantly, it needs to know what you've already typed. It takes these partial queries to return additional suggestions. It's a powerful way to add keyword terms to your list that you might have missed before.

Here's another way you can add new discoveries to your master list. Try sites like Synonyms.net and Synonym.com to generate words of similar meaning to something you've already chosen. Of course using a printed thesaurus can produce similar results too. In fact, you might be pleasantly surprised how this simple step can help grow your keyword list and get more traffic from your articles. Go ahead and put it to the test.

Join groups and visit forums related to your target market. Pay attention to the questions being asked, as well as the language used. Look at the titles of popular posts. Do any of these give you ideas for additional keyword terms you can add to your growing list?

If you're not sure where to find discussion boards related to your market, visit big-boards.com or boardtracker.com. These sites can help you find the niche market discussions you're after. Conversely, you can always type your root keyword, followed by the term "forum" or "discussion board" to discover where people in your market tend to hang out online.

Refine and Revise Your Keyword List to Hit Gold

Only after you've compiled a massive list is it time to prioritize your top selections and create a miniature list of keywords you'll want to get started quickly. Look for the best opportunities. That means looking for keyword combo's that ideally fit your market and business, but without having too much search competition already established.

You can conduct your search for the "low-hanging fruit" fruit using Google's free keyword tool, or you can speed up the process and head straight to those golden keywords with the help of a proven keyword tool many online marketers rave about.

Long-tail keywords should be your primary focus. These terms have much lower search volumes, but you'll find it much easier to rank high for these terms. Use plenty of long-tail keywords and try to rank high for each. By default, the search engines will elevate your listings for the more general terms too.

The more articles you distribute centered upon very specific long-tail keyword phrases, the more of an "authority" you tend to become in the online search world. This can only help you through added exposure and opportunities.

With a huge keyword list in hand, it's easy to spot the ones that will be easy to write. Thumb through your list and you'll see what I mean. Some keywords will stump you. Others will leap off the page, calling you to write something about them.

Add a small check-mark to any that grab your attention right off the bat. Here's another article writing tip that can help: should any title come to mind as you consider possible keyword terms, go ahead and record it next to the keyword that best fits into your title. Capturing ideas and angles as they come to you is an excellent technique for getting a jump on your article writing.

The Secret About Long-Tail Keywords

Your greatest challenge with article keywords is to find the ideal match to reach these people as they're thinking those very thoughts.

Far more searches are carried out using broad search terms, at least in the beginning stages. So the numbers are way more impressive with root keywords than with any narrowly-defined derivative. But long-tail terms tend to attract the more serious, got-to-have-it-now information seekers.

These are often the folks who are quick to become buyers. Since they know what they want, they're more apt to snag it when they see it. Your long-tail optimized article provides a direct path to any page on your site and the closer the match between search term and what you offer - the greater your ability to turn a profit from your articles or content pages.

Using long-tail keyword terms mean that it's easier to rank higher in the search engines. If you're lucky, you can get front-page listings for some keyword terms easily because there's often (but not always) very little competition. Typically, you just can't beat the value of these top listings, as long as enough people are using the exact same keyword term to seek out additional details on your subject.

Using a selected long-tail keyword term inside a headline-style title makes the link to your article leap off the page of search results, taking the visitor straight to your article.

The more "Page One" listings you have in the major engines, the greater the value of your web property. Every page is a potential customer magnet and therefore, an asset in its own right, although listings change and rankings vary. But every incoming link and every lead-generating article that draws your prospects in, adds value to your own virtual real estate. This is an important consideration should you ever decide to sell your web site down the road.

When you focus on building your articles around specific long-tail keyword terms, you're taking a grass roots approach to building your asset. It starts with a single article and a trickle of traffic. But each one generates a little more exposure. Pretty soon you've got a whole army of long-tail keyword optimized articles all doing their part in attracting a few qualified eyeballs here and there. Collectively it increases your traffic exponentially. Those trickles of traffic combined mean a significant volume of visitors and this is something the search engines notice. Suddenly you'll find your articles ranking much higher for your root keywords as well. After all, many of your long-tail keyword combo's will contain a variation of a major root keyword.

Feature mostly long-tail keyword terms in your articles and your results will continue to roll in. Spread your marketing efforts wide and take whatever streams of traffic you can get. Build on it by adding more articles all related to your major market.

Go wide first and you'll deepen your market penetration automatically.

Write and submit multiple articles on various sub-topics within your market. Utilize every long-tail keyword variation you can find - even those with hardly any searches. Dominate those listings and the search engines will reward you by sending more visitors to your site.

How To Get More People To Read Your Article

Your title is the single most important part of any article you write. After all, it's the first thing anyone sees. So it's worth it to pay extra attention to your titles and test various approaches.

It's the title that determines which way your prospect goes. If the title succeeds in generating interest, fuelling intrigue, or arousing curiosity, your article stands a chance of wooing prospects inside. In other words, you've got to make it sound appealing to get people to at least take a look at your article. If your title isn't doing the job - try revising it.

If your title doesn't pull interested readers inside, you've lost out forever on attracting those eyeballs to your article.

Search engine listings begin with a single line in bold text that contains the first part, if not the entire title. Directory listings are scanned at hyper-speed until prospects find that one title that reels them in. However your articles appear, it's the title that either stops people in their tracks and pulls them in, or sends them searching for what they want some other place.

Visitors to your site scan content in much the same way. They're looking for a reason to go beyond the headlines. If you have a page listing nothing but titles and you've hyper-linked these to your complete articles, you'll find that certain ones will command greater interest than others. Some will get clicked on far more than others.

Why?

It's due to the title and nothing else because that's all your visitors have to work with. So they base their decision on the title. Sure, where exactly in sequence a title appears on a list is likely a factor too, particularly with large article collections. But the number one reason some articles get read far more than others listed on the same page is due to the pulling power of the title - and nothing more.

Do Your Titles Capture Attention and Interest?

Your title is much like a headline in advertising. It's the headline that calls out to targeted prospects… stops them cold… intensifies their interest… and welcomes them inside where they can get all the juicy details. Article titles command the same kind of power.

It's the title that is always the first thing a potential reader notices. It's the title they first stumble upon and it's this one brief line of text alone that determines their direction.

Each new title represents a crossroad in the reader's trail -- and most just speed right on through. But your title has the opportunity and the capability to direct them down your road.

Prospects must make a decision at this fork in the road and there are really only two ways they could go. Readers can:

1. Take a pass and continue their search for specific information... or they can...

2. Continue reading your article.

If they move on, your title failed the test.

But if they click through and continue reading your piece, the title you chose did the exact job it was supposed to do.

Earliest impressions are conveyed through titles. It's the first point of contact between you and anyone who happens to come across your material in their online travels. It doesn't matter whether it is content from an article directory, posted on a blog, or right on your site. It's the title that dictates the direction people take because they're on a mission to discover specific information.

You've got just a split second to make a favourable impression and cast a strong enough magnetic pull to draw people in. Impressions are created on the spot and decisions are made faster than ever in the online search for information. Therefore, it's the title that represents your greatest point of power.

In an instant, you title appears on the screen of an individual user. What happens next depends on the relevancy of the match between what the prospect wants and what your title promises to deliver and the effectiveness of the delivery of that message in the title. Strive for attention and interest with every article headline you write.

Make Your Title Stand Out

There's no end to the number of choices available online today. Every search - even of a very specific kind - serves up a bounty of choices. But what makes people choose one link over another? It's the appeal, power, relevancy and impact of the title or headline.

You've got to make your title stand out. If it gets buried amidst a flurry of competing articles, all your efforts to write a strong article will be in vain.

Titles that speak softly tend to go unnoticed. I'm not suggesting that you shout out your titles with the Caps Lock engaged, or figuratively scream out obnoxiously like some advertising headlines do. But you've got to be noticed to gain a readership. So you've got to make your title as dominant and irresistible as you can, using nothing but the power of your words.

The easiest way to make your article title appealing is to deliver a significant benefit. Not just any benefit, but one you know your specific audience wants. Promise something your reader desires and you'll get her attention. Make it riveting and compelling and she'll continue reading. That's exactly what you want, since the only way you can benefit is if they first read the article and then click on the link in your resource box.

Easy Plug and Play Article Title Formats That Work Like Magic

When it comes to choosing an article title format, the options are many. Simple lists make an excellent format for articles. "5 Ways To _____" (Insert any specific benefit) - is an easy article to write in any market. All you have to do is make a list of tips, ways, secrets, methods, or shortcuts and write a sentence or two about each.

This is also the kind of article title that draws a high readership because it suggests easy reading and a bullet-point or numbered-list style that is easy to scoop information from.

Lists are also effective because they suggest easy steps or methods that are effective in helping readers achieve a specific, desired result.

"How to" articles are another favourite. This type of article headline suggests a process for the accomplishment of a particular task, or the attainment of sought-after solution or result. Here are a few examples:

How To Groom Your Dog at Home Like a Pro
How To Legally Slash the Amount of Income Tax You Pay This Year
How To Do Your Own Car Detailing and Save Yourself $150 Every Time
Do-It-Yourself Lawn Care: How To Make Your Property Look Like a Golf Course
How To Double Your Reading Speed Overnight With One Simple Technique

It's an offer of assistance or guidance about how to go about doing something to get more… to get it faster… to do it better… or to get it done cheaper… and so on. The "How to" article provides expertise and insight. It infers that the information comes from someone in the know. It's an "insider" sharing information from their perspective. Or it could be someone with personal experience that they're willing to share to help others accomplish the same kind of outcome.

"Question" titles tend to pull readers inside. This is completely natural, since we're all conditioned from a very young age to answer questions as they're asked. Go check it out right now. Ask the nearest person a question - any question - and watch the process at work. To not answer in automatic fashion takes conscious effort. It's the same thing with titles phrased as questions directed at targeted readers. People are compelled to answer, or to find the answers. They want to know the answer and to see if they were correct with their response. Examples include:

Do You Make These Mistakes When Planting Seedlings?
Looking For a Second Income Stream From Home?
What Are The Early Warning Signs of Heart Disease?
Is Green Tea Really As Healthy As Some People Think?
Are Your Kids At Risk of Graduating 8th Grade Without These Vital Life Skills?

Questions are powerful lures that people are conditioned to respond to. Every question begs to be answered. That's just the way we've been conditioned to react. That's why it often requires greater mental energy to avoid question-style titles than to click through and discover the answers revealed in the body copy.

You can also use questions to set up a "how to" presentation of your information. In this case, a question title can help set the stage for what follows. Another approach is to use a question in your opening sentence. It helps stir reader interest so they continue along.

Yet another approach is to create intrigue. Add an element of mystery to your title by revealing an unusual source of your information. It's this kind of twist that arouses curiosity, which in turn can make all the difference in the numbers of people who access your article.

Here are some examples of interesting twists:

3 Things I Learned About People Management From My Daughter's 5th Grade Class
Ancient Selling Secrets and How To Make Them Work Just As Well Today
Natural Skin-Nourishing Tips Discovered In The Desert

Controversy is another way to stand out and lure in large volumes of readers. Take a position on something that contradicts common acceptance or belief. Be sure you stay on course and deliver the kind of information readers seek. But don't hesitate to toss a little controversy into the mix to. Take a position designed to stir things up. Challenge your reader to meet you inside where they can get to see where you're coming from.

Here are few idea-starters for injecting controversy into your article title:

Nutrient-Enriched Potatoes Turn Chips Into Health Food
How Women Control The Economy In Good Times and Bad
Reading Is For Losers Says Video Training Expert

What's the easiest way to learn how to create eye-appealing titles? Learn from magazines sold in retail stores and at newsstands. Any consumer publication that relies on point-of-purchase sales needs to employ powerful headlines or article titles on every cover.

Take any magazine like Men's Health, Cosmopolitan, or Prevention and you'll see what I mean. Look at the tabloids like USA Today and National Enquirer too. You'll find covers and front pages loaded with titles that act as headlines to capture the attention and interest of more readers.

Visit the newspaper and magazine racks of the largest bookstore you can find in your community. Take a small notepad with you and jot down headlines from the covers of the dominant consumer magazines. Or you can view various magazine covers online at Amazon or Magazines.com.

Either method serves the purpose. Observing the kind of article titles magazine and tabloid publishers use to grab more eyeballs is an education in itself. And it's a great way to build a "swipe file" of effective titles that you can later modify for your own articles.

Below are some examples I found today by viewing the latest editions of several consumer publications. As you scan through this list, think of how you might be able to use a similar title for your articles.

From Woman's Health...

Drop Two Sizes in Just Two Weeks

Success Without Distress Discover a Happier, Healthier You

Hot Sex News - Kick Your Sex Life Up a Notch

15 Fat Burning Power Foods

More Energy - Instantly

Lose Your Belly! Weight Loss Secrets That Work

From CondeNast Traveller...

Best Islands! 37 Easy Escapes

Affordable Hawaii 6 Islands, 22 Stays Under $200

Ultimate Greek Island Finder - 20 Top Isles For Beaches, Beauty, Hotels and More

Spain's Sexy New Star

India's Secret Paradise

From Prevention...

Feel 10 Years Younger! 6 New Tips Inspired by "The Biggest Loser"

Fire Up Fat Loss - Flip Your Metabolism Switch - New Plan Boosts Fat Burn 50%

21 Health Signs To Never Ignore

Sleep Deeply Every Night (And Wake Up Happy!)

Eat To Unleash Energy

Flatten Your Belly Faster

From Vogue...

Spring Goes Sexy - Daring Jumpsuits Smoldering Makeup Plunging Necklines

Vitamin D - The Healthy Side of Sunshine

Blake Lively - The Gossip Girl Star's New Look

More Magical Makeovers - From the White House To a Fashion Empire

Newman's Own – Paul's Daughter On Her Father's Legacy

Simple Luxuries - Balancing Your Clothing and Beauty Budgets

From Money...

How To Thrive In A Bad Economy

The 15 Best Investments For Income Now

What Obama Means For Your Money

Sane Strategies For A Crazed Market

6 Ways To Bulletproof Your Job

The Sweetest Deal in Real Estate

From Men's Health...

What Winners Know - 6 Smart Strategies You Need Right Now

Spring Guide To Style

14 Moves That Define a Man

Men's Wealth - Build It, Protect It, Enjoy It

Great Food Guaranteed - Your 'Eat This, Not That!' Supermarket Survival Guide

The Woman Whisperer - 5 Ways To Get (And Keep) Her Attention

Stop Target Readers Cold With A Title That Connects

Powerful article titles often target their audience. They tip off searchers as to whom the article was written for. Let's face it – every article has a limited audience. You're writing articles within a specific niche market, so anyone outside of that market is not likely interested in what you or anyone else has to say about it.

When you address a group like work-at-home moms, or scrapbook enthusiasts, you're speaking to a specific audience. Even though you might be sharing practical business tips, your article is slanted to a narrowly-defined group. Therefore, any outsiders will steer clear. They simply filter you out and pass by your title. This is as it should be.

You want to attract only those who fit the profile of someone who could become your customer. No sense trying to attract everybody. In marketing (which is what you're doing by writing and posting hundreds of different articles) "everybody" really means nobody. Instead, set your sights on those within your market and then target these prospects right in your title.

Here are a few examples of article titles that directly target a specific reader:

7 Deck-Building Tips For The Do-It-Yourselfer
The Single-Parents 3-Step Guide To Raising Happy, Productive Children
For Dog Lovers Only: 5 Healthy Ways To Show Your Love

Communicate succinctly what your article reveals. Every effective title conveys enough information at a glance about the specific topic, so potential readers can make an instantaneous decision. Disguising your real topic is a disservice to readers and it probably won't help you much in the long run. Tell them what you've got. Then deliver it.

Think of your title as a label for your article. What's your piece all about? How would you sum up your article in just a few words? What can you say about your topic that's certain to capture attention?

Readers want content. But they won't get to your content if your title doesn't draw them inside. And if they start reading and find that the content is a mismatch to the title, they're most likely to abandon your piece straight away. It's important to make your title inviting. But it's equally important to accurately depict your article's content.

Condense key points into a short summary about your topic. Tell your reader what your article is about within the article title itself. Create a title that intrigues and excites. Give viewers a quick overview of the benefits served up in the text that follows. Provide a basis or framework for your story and do so in as interesting a way as possible.

Strong Article Titles Help Spark Your Target Prospect's Interest

Think of your title as the sign or window display of a store. Is it inviting... descriptive... specific... or intriguing? Or does it assume the reader will automatically be compelled to step inside? Don't take potential readers for granted. Instead, turn every title into a workhouse that attracts maximum numbers of qualified prospects.

Imagine that you were in a position where you had to sell your home. You want to get the best possible price, considering all the upgrades and improvements you've made. Inside, your house is an amazing place with every creature comfort imaginable. Get potential buyers inside and you know they'll love it and will want to put in an offer right away.

But there's one big problem.

On the outside, your house doesn't look like much. Oh you planned to get to all those things like painting, installing a new garage door and adding a touch of professional landscaping. But it's winter. So you've chosen to wait until spring for those tasks.

Unfortunately, first impressions make a big impact. The outside appearance of the home is like the title of your article. If the title looks inviting, interested parties will go further. But the opposite is also true. A lacklustre, ho-hum, rundown, or uninviting title won't get you the readership you seek.

With the bounty of choices available, hundreds of other options are just a click away. Everyone online knows that.

But as your visitor's experience grows, they come to realize that much of what is found, initially at least, is not really what they wanted. So as they scan through search engine results or article directories, your prospects are actually looking for reasons to disqualify your article. The slightest, split-second signal keeps them moving along. But when they find a headline that hits them between the eyes and grabs their attention, they're all over it like a curious kitten that has just discovered a big ball of wool.

More on the Value of Effective Titles

If your information is superior, don't shy away from giving it an appropriate title like "The Ultimate (Target Market's) Action Plan To...". If it's speed and simplicity you want to get across, consider a title like "The 90-Second Guide To...".

You want to capture the attention of the maximum number of your best target prospects. These are the people you want to draw to your site and invite into your marketing funnel. There's no sense in firing blindfolded, hoping to get lucky and hit your target.

Address your market directly. "Article Marketers: 5 Secrets To..." singles out a specific target reader. Or clarify your intended audience within the context itself: "4 Easy and Additional Ways To Grow Your Business By Writing Articles".

Provide an overview of your subject matter in an appealing way. You need to get the general idea of your article across quickly. If you skirt the subject matter in an attempt to lure more prospects, you may get more initial visits, but most of those visitors won't be genuine prospects.

Anyone who doesn't fit your prospect profile is of little or no value to you. So attracting unqualified page views is meaningless. That's why it's always a good idea to convey the subject matter in your title, or at least tip off readers in advance of having them land at your site when it's not really what they wanted in the first place.

This way, anyone opening your full article does so out of genuine interest in the topic. This approach beats the heck out of a blind title that lures curious readers, only to disappoint them later when the true subject is revealed.

Readers want benefits - so serve yours up in generous portions. Communicate what the reader wants to know and they'll be drawn to you and your article.

How To Start Off With a Bang

So you've chosen a topic to write about. You've mapped out a basic outline that indicates in a general way, the material you'll be covering. And by now you've got a title that works for you too. All that's left is to write the article and add your promotional link at the end. It can be a challenge the first few times. But once you've written several articles, it gets a whole lot easier.

Now, here's how to start your article off with a thunderous roar.

Selecting your topic and title are important, preliminary steps. But how do you move forward to write the actual article?

For many would-be article writers, they've just run into another wall. Even with the most ambitious of intentions, getting started on the writing part can be a hang-up. It's a definite sticking point for some. But you can't allow it to stop you.

My advice is to jump right in and start writing.

Use one of the article opening templates in this book to kick-start the writing process for you. All you have to do is take any template and fill in the blanks.

Get the first sentence down and you're off and running. Once you get rolling, momentum will carry you. It's like being at the top of a snow-covered hill on a toboggan. Sometimes you need just a gentle push to get started. But once you begin the descent, moving ever so slowly, your ride to the finish line becomes a quick trip that goes by in a flash.

Some article writers find it easiest to leave the introduction until the basic article is complete. They then introduce the topic, or frame it exactly as the information is presented in the body copy. You may find that writing your introductions last makes it easier on you. Instead of imagining how your article will take shape and trying to set the stage in advance, writing it afterward can make introducing the value or ultimate benefit by way of your introduction, that much easier.

I prefer to start at the beginning and build each article one sentence at a time, from start to finish. It boosts productivity and helps keep me channelled in a single direction; one that's in alignment with the intended topic. I also find it easier to follow the process in an orderly, step-by-step fashion.

Jumping around from section to section tends to slow production, at least for me. Once you've written several articles in a row, you'll get a better sense for whatever method works best for you. Stick with whatever gives you the best results and discard what doesn't.

How To Write An Introduction: The Purpose of The First Paragraph

Opening paragraphs are crucial to the success of your articles because they provide an entry point. It's this brief introduction that launches the article. The opening or lead merely informs the reader of what's in store.

Here's an easy way to carry on where the title left off: write your opening paragraph as a more detailed sub-heading to your title.

The best way to explain this is by example. Let's say your article topic is "Walking For Weight Loss". So your title might be something like this:

"How To Walk Your Way to Easy and Natural Weight Loss" and your introduction could be something like this...

"If easy and natural weight loss is important to you, read on. I'm going to show you how to melt fat without sweating through your clothes, without spending hours at the gym and without forking over hundreds of dollars in membership fees. Walking is nature's solution to weight loss. But it only works when you follow a few simple but proven ideas."

To use this technique, think of your title as a main headline on a sales letter. Then follow it up with a supporting sub-head that further fuels the interest of the reader you've already targeted. It's a one-two punch that intensifies the interest of those captive eyeballs. A strong title captures the reader's attention and the introduction confirms and expands upon it.

Introductions set the stage for readers. It helps them to focus by providing direction and a brief warm-up before you unleash your main article content. It's important however that you don't wander or spit out unnecessary words endlessly. Stay on target and keep it brief. Make every word justify its presence - just as you would in a headline or classified ad.

It's the introduction that sets up the main idea and gives a short title meaning – while it helps readers understand your message. The title jumps out and invites them inside. And the introduction adds depth and context. It's this opening that gives you a paragraph or two to explain your position.

You've got lots more space to supply plenty of enticing details that you couldn't fit into the title itself.

Good openings create anticipation. Your prospects were first drawn by the title. Now it's your chance to build up their interest by hinting at the big payoff still to come.

Creating anticipation means prospects will stay tuned. Anything less and they'll quickly grow bored and the moment that happens, they'll dash away immediately.

Pull In a Larger Audience With an Opening That Engages and Leads The Reader

Stop and think about this for a moment. Ideally, every paragraph of your article - in fact every sentence - leads the reader to the next one. You've got to connect with your audience and share the kind of information that will keep them interested, mentally occupied and fully engaged.

Your goal should be to provide useful content. That's the number one key if you want to make short and sweet articles payoff. In so doing, you encourage others to take action by clicking on the link provided. But they'll never get near that link at the bottom of the page if you fail to engage them in the very early stages.

Connecting with your reader means writing about what's important to them. It's never about you, your product, your service or your business. It's always about sharing something that's of benefit, interest and value to the reader.

You have to make it interesting, intriguing, or promising enough to carry them through the complete text of your article. Any break in the path and they'll fall through the cracks and when that happens, all your efforts are soon wasted.

Open the discussion in your introductory paragraph. It's probably not a good idea to give up the gold just yet. But you can place the spade in their hand and reveal the map to the buried treasure.

Tempt your target prospects to read your entire article to get it all, instead of revealing your biggest secret right away. Build up to it. Not in a meandering or fluff-filled way, but in a way that keeps those eyeballs glued to the page.

Share your expertise. Show that you know what you're talking about and readers will want to connect with you to learn even more.

Giving up rock-solid information suggests that there's plenty more where that came from. Readers will want to visit your site, sign up for your newsletter, buy your products and otherwise connect with you when you first connect with them by sharing your inside knowledge and experience.

Quick and Easy Opening Paragraph Formats That Work

Looking for some quick and easy article writing shortcuts? Great - here you go. This method makes creating an introduction a breeze. Employing a question is one proven approach to writing an introduction. As prospects land on the page, you hit them up with something that gets them to think. Make it a question that immediately involves them in the mini lesson presented in the text.

Here are a few "idea starters" for using the question technique:

If you knew the one secret to...
How often have you said to yourself...
What if you could...
What would happen if...
Have you ever...
Whoever said _____ must not have...

Or, you could ask a specific question readers want to know.

"Want to know the real secret to losing weight easily and naturally - without expensive equipment, memberships, or supplements?"

This kind of on-target question can quickly pull readers inside. Of course getting them there is only part of the puzzle. You'll need to deliver on the promise in order to trigger the action you want your readers to take.

A quick story that hits home can also quickly build a connection between you and your target audience. Here's an example:

"Losing the 25 extra pounds of fat I dragged around for years was an impossible task. I hated being overweight and feeling sluggish all the time. I tried everything from diet shakes to working out at the gym 5 days a week. And I bought every new gadget that came along because if it worked even half as good as it did for the folks in the commercial, I would be fat-free at last.

But it wasn't until I stopped the diet merry-go-round and gave away every piece of exercise equipment I ever accumulated that I started to shed those unwanted pounds. Turns out I didn't need any of that stuff anyway. All I needed was to do what my body was designed to do. Soon after I started walking every day, I couldn't believe my eyes."

See how this simple story can work to pull readers inside?

That's all it takes to deliver an adequate "set-up" for your material. It doesn't require two or three paragraphs either. Can you tell a story that readers will instantly connect with in one paragraph? Then by all means, do so. It's only the introduction you're writing at this point, so don't get too carried away.

Tell your story - but keep it short and sweet. Just be sure to engage your audience before unveiling the information you want to share in your article.

Startling facts and statistics can be powerful grabbers too. Share a piece of information and quote the source to add credibility to what you're relaying to your readers. Get to the heart of it right away. Don't quote a long paragraph from a research study. Instead summarize what is most significant about this information to your readers.

Press release sites can be useful sources or interesting news, surprising facts and relevant information. You can find plenty of press release distribution sites buy searching the web.

Also, check out the media room or press resources page of major research companies. Research companies earn revenue by researching, compiling and publishing information. But they need to publicize their information to make people aware of it. Many of these firms rely on press releases to get the word out. You can find valuable snippets of information you can use for your articles by visiting the websites of organizations like:

Forrester Research (www.forrester.com)
Frost & Sullivan (www.frost.com)
Marketdata Enterprises (www.marketdataenterprises.com)
Simba Information (www.simbainformation.com)
Yankelovich (www.yankelovich.com)

Another approach is to set the scene in advance. The thinking here is to meet the reader where they are. In other words, connect with the ongoing thoughts and concerns of your audience to capture their attention and draw readers in. Here's an example following the earlier theme of weight loss:

"So you've set your goal with the best of intentions. You know you can lose the extra weight with a regular program of jogging. So you bought the best shoes you could find and now you're ready. As 6am approaches and the alarm sounds, that's when it hits you. You need a bigger reason than new shoes to crawl out of a warm bed and hit the streets."

An alternate method of creating an introduction is to state your thesis and then expand upon it. What's the core information promised in your title? All you have to do is take that information and say it another way. If your subject is "Building Web Pages Fast", you can open your article with something like…

"Building web pages quickly is easier than ever. What used to require the services of an experienced web designer with access to expensive software can now be accomplished by just about anyone with a computer and internet connection. In this article, I'm going to show you how you can build your own pages lightning-fast - without spending a fortune."

Sounding an alarm is a sure-fire way to command attention. Hit your reader with relevant data from a survey, poll, or news story. Or you can reveal how out of control a particular problem can be by adding a splash of color. Here's an example:

"It's shocking! In fact, it makes you wonder how 'big business' gets away with it. The dangers of some packaged foods are clear. And yet in the time it takes you to read this article, thousands of parents will fill their shopping carts with foods that are actually harming their children."

Actual experiences of users can establish a powerful introduction to your article. In terms of article writing shortcuts, this method can pack quite a punch. Think about what could be relevant in that experience to your readers. Then capture its essence quickly and dramatically.

The following example illustrates this concept:

"Yesterday I heard from an inner-circle member who told me about his 'silly little twist' to my system that earned him an extra $67k last year. This new angle should interest everyone who ever thought about starting a part-time business to create extra income. Here are the 5 different steps Lance used to turn one income stream into a raging cash river."

5 Key Points To Remember When Writing An Article Introduction

There are plenty of ways to write an introduction. Your task is to make it as compelling as you can without spending too much time. After all, the introduction is just one segment of your piece. So set your lead quickly and complete your article fast. Then write another in quick succession.

Helping you write multiple articles that serve you is my objective. So don't get bogged down with any single part of the article equation – there's no need. Any stoppage or slowdown only limits your output. I've provided you with some quick-start introduction templates at the back of the book.

But first, let's look at five key points to keep in mind when writing article introductions:

1. Keep It Short. Make your article look like an easy read by breaking up larger paragraphs into smaller ones. It's a good idea at this point to think of your article as a sales letter. All successful sales letters use this idea. They start out as easy reading. The opening paragraph of your article should also invite and entice readers, so that anyone landing there automatically continues reading. Make your text inviting by easing readers into it. Never start with your largest paragraph. Shorten it up. Then make it even shorter if you can. If it's easy to get started, odds are they will continue.

2. Stay On Target. Make sure that the content is a good fit to your title. Your title did the job of delivering readers. Now it's time to turn on the jets to crank up interest a few notches higher. Suggest the payoff that readers can get only one way - by continuing to read your content.

3. Unveil Your Greatest Benefit. Begin to take the wraps off your information. But don't fully expose your best idea in the first paragraph, or they may not read on. Instead suggest what they'll get by continuing down the page.

4. Think of Your Lead Paragraph As An Introductory Handshake. Is it weak and limp... overpowering and domineering... or just right? Make yours firm so that it conveys a strong sense of confidence and knowledge. That's the kind of power a strong opening wields. It can make or break the relationship with your prospect. If you've attracted readers this far, they're obviously a good match for your information. But whether they stay or go depends on how inviting and appealing you make your information and presentation.

5. Make a Promise To Your Reader. State your case, or your position. Tell readers what you're about to share in your article introduction and then set out to do just that in the most interesting and direct way. Then stay on track and work at retaining your reader's interest.

Article Content Secrets: How To Create The Body Copy of Your Article Faster Than Ever

Your body copy is the heart and soul of every piece you write. It's where you deliver your article content - the information readers want. It's where you share all the details pertaining to the subject of your chosen topic.

The body or text of your article is the largest single component. It can vary from a couple of paragraphs to several pages in length, depending on your publishing intentions. For our purposes here, we'll stick to the short article formula of between 350 and 750 words.

Just to give you a quick point of reference, the above paragraph is 79 words. This means that just 4 paragraphs of the same length would give you an article of 316 words. That may be on the smaller side of the article scale, but it may certainly be enough to post to a blog.

Let's assume that your introduction and conclusion are each one paragraph in length. If each contained just 75 words, your body copy would only require a minimum of 350 additional words for a 500-word article. This means that with just the 3-4 paragraphs directly above, plus a 75-word introduction and another 75-word conclusion (essentially the set-up for a resource box) you would probably have enough (or nearly enough) content to qualify as a genuinely helpful and informative article.

Now, you'll want to be sure to give readers enough information to quench their initial thirst for details. And you have to deliver on the promise of the title. So be sure to provide value. But by the same token, you're not writing a book. Share something significant and then move on to the next one.

The point is… it doesn't take a ton of time, effort, or words to compose an article. And in many cases, it may be more effective for you to write two or more separate articles instead of one monster article.

You never want to purposely chop an article into pieces. Each needs to stand on its own and convey a specific message. But if you plan your article writing strategy to mostly focus on shorter articles, you'll boost your published article numbers, your exposure and your traffic. And the cost in terms of time and effort is virtually the same.

Leveraging your time as a writer is one of the big keys to high-output content creation. Think of each article as one tool out in the marketplace working for you. It's a lead-generating mechanism designed to attract suitable prospects to your site.

Paying customers are the lifeblood of any business. But every customer is first a prospect. Articles placed online can work like prospect magnets, pulling fresh new leads to you, twenty-four hours a day.

The Secret To Maximum Writing Productivity

Here's a strategy that will help you sail through your article writing sessions with energy and enthusiasm. We touched on this earlier, but I want to explain it in more detail now. You'll create more articles with greater ease and speed than you ever thought possible with this writing productivity secret.

It's the concept of learning to think in three's: three ideas… three tips… three ways… three paragraphs.

If you can do that, you can jump right in and join the most prolific article writers out there.

The idea is to flesh out enough detail to meet the minimum as a first step. That means three simple ideas… or three points. Remember, just three basic paragraphs, along with some introductory and concluding comments and you've probably met the requirements of an article. Of course you can always add to it if necessary or desirable to do so.

Essentially what I want you to take from this is the idea of "thinking in three's". Nothing will boost your article writing productivity more than this little concept. All you have to do is come up with three details related to your subject and then write a paragraph about each. Your "big three" could take the form of…

- 3 tips
- 3 questions that always come up
- 3 most important things
- 3 points
- 3 pitfalls

Take any of the above examples and simply plug in 3 items or answers. It can be quick and easy - as well as fun. You'll be delighted with your surge in productivity when you become accustomed to using this method to generate content ideas for your articles.

For a simple outline that works, a single word or phrase is usually adequate to start. Then expand each of the three steps, secrets, pitfalls – or whatever – into a paragraph or two. Insert a basic opening and add a close and you're basically done. That's the beauty of "thinking in three's". It's quick and easy to come up with content in just seconds. And that's exactly what you need to become a highly-efficient article writing machine.

Can you break your subject down into 3 basic steps?

If so, all you have to do is list each of these in sequential order and write a couple of sentences describing each of the three steps in the process. First you do this… then you do that… and finally this step will help you get to where you want to go. It's an A-B-C formula for article writing that's super easy to follow.

Beware of any sequence that has too many steps, or your article will require more time to write. There's nothing inherently wrong with this and you may find good uses for longer, step-by-step articles such as converting them into reports, or posting them directly to your site. But often it makes more sense to take the content of a larger or more complex step-by-step process and break it down into multiple articles.

Another Method For Creating Unique Articles Quickly and Easily

Since the body copy is the heart and soul of quality, unique articles, that's where the largest chunk of your writing time is spent. Providing a fresh angle means that every piece is a completely original article.

You are free to move in any direction you wish with article writing. Every article you write will be yours and yours alone if you use these ideas to stimulate your unlimited creative mind. Don't just write what everyone else does. Add your own points, personality and perspective. This alone will set you apart.

Below are some additional "thought triggers" to stimulate your creativity and help you uncover three key elements instantly. Use them and you'll find new angles for additional articles.

Any one of these idea-generators can be the catalyst that gets you going on a new article for your blog, web site, or to post in an article directory or elsewhere online. Try different variations. Choose one method that works for you and use it to generate multiple ideas from that one method. Once you get on a roll, let momentum carry you.

Here are a few samples to get you started:

1. What are the first three ideas that come to mind when you think of this topic? (Simply jot down the words, ideas, thoughts, or images that appear on the screen of your mind.)

2. Divide your topic into three by looking at the past, present and future. How was the task completed in the past? How are today's methods different? How will the future change the way things are done today? (Identify the before... the now... and how it might be in years to come and write a paragraph about each.)

3. What are the first three steps to take to get you on the right track to accomplish a task or obtain a result? (What actions will move readers closer to the outcome they seek?)

4. What are the most common mistakes in this area? (Identify where most people get it wrong and then show your readers how to get it right.)

I've given you some ideas to prompt your inner creativity. Once you're tapped in and turned on creatively, you'll find an endless stream of content ideas to use.

Now you just need to plug in the content that fits. That's your job as niche marketer, topic expert or specialist in your chosen field. And it's why it's important to gain a foundational understanding and immerse the mind in the subject at hand as a preliminary step.

Life as an article writer and marketer is so much easier when you have a genuine interest in the overall topic or niche. Surround yourself with the best sources of information and soak it up like a sponge in water. Then use the triggers presented here to tap into that vast reservoir of information and answers inside you.

How To Write An Article Conclusion That Does The Job

Typically, the conclusion is nothing more than a closing statement. It's a brief summary of the information you previously covered in the text. But in the case of articles on another site, your conclusion - in fact your entire article - needs to lead the reader to take the action step and click on the link provided in the resource box.

Wikipedia defines it this way: "A conclusion is a proposition which is arrived at after the consideration of evidence, arguments or logic".

You've just presented your case. Now the conclusion hammers it home.

Think of the conclusion as your closing argument. It's a natural and logical point of arrival after the presentation of ideas. It's the expected, sequential "conclusion" of the information you just finished sharing. Now it's just a matter of getting the desired action.

Your conclusion might include a quick point summary of the material as a reminder. It could be as simple as recapping your three main points: "Step one is this. Step two is that. And finally, step three completes the process. Take all three steps in this order you will get the results you seek."

Next, your resource box jumps right out and leads readers to the pot of gold they seek.

Summarize a few specific steps the reader can take to make the most of the content you just shared. Make your information actionable and then inspire them to accomplishment. Simply remind your readers what to do first, second and third in order to complete the task you just detailed in your article. The more meaningful and informative your content is, the greater the odds of getting the click.

Give readers something they can take action on and you will be delivering information of value. Value is the key. You want people to go beyond your conclusion. You want to create such a favourable impression that they take further action by visiting your site or blog and signing up for your newsletter, or purchasing your product right away.

Think of your article as a short speech and present your material accordingly. Following the often stated, refined version of Aristotle's thoughts on the topic:

1. Tell 'em what you're going to tell 'em.

2. Tell 'em.

3. Tell 'em what you told 'em.

The first part is delivered in the introduction. Then in the body of your article, you "tell them". And finally you use the conclusion to review what you've just covered and gently lead them to the next step. That's all there is to it.

As you wind down your article, emphasize for your reader the important points and the kind of results they can expect by following your advice. Don't just give valuable information. Remind readers of the essential tidbits and how they can put these exact ideas to work for themselves.

Concluding paragraphs come easier after you've written several dozen of them. Remember to keep it simple. There's no need whatsoever for a conclusion that rambles on endlessly. That will only produce the opposite of what you want. No need to be excessively wordy here. Just get right to it and move readers through your content straight to the resource box and your link.

Like many aspects of article writing, getting started on your conclusion segment can be a drag. Sometimes it's the biggest hurdle of all. But if you can clear that one, the rest of the track is downhill. It's easy once you get rolling. But getting started in a way that sounds right to you can quickly bring your article marketing efforts to a screeching halt.

To help you through it and to ensure that you don't stand idly by when your article is only a paragraph away from being completed, I've prepared some "starter conclusions" and will cover those next.

How To Write Super-Fast Conclusions in Seconds

If you struggle with article writing, chances are it's because there are a number of hurdles to climb with each article you craft. First, you need a title. The next element is the introduction, soon followed by body copy. And finally, there's the conclusion and resource box.

That's five different components for one article. No wonder it can be a little daunting for some to write articles consistently.

Like the other aspects of article writing, banging out a conclusion can be a drag. In fact, sometimes it's the biggest hurdle of all, because you've already written the content, but it seems incomplete without an effective conclusion. Clear this hurdle before it becomes a major obstacle and you'll find it a lot easier to keep those articles coming on a regular basis.

To help you from getting stuck when your article is only one short paragraph away from completion, here are several starters to help get you going:

1. There you have it...
2. As you can see...
3. As you've just discovered...
4. When in doubt, simply...
5. You now know how to...
6. Shocking? Perhaps. But...

7. Surprised how easy it can be? Go ahead and...
8. There's no question...
9. Imagine getting the same kind of...
10. Just think where you would be today if you had this kind of information...
11. I know this can work for you because...
12. That's all there is to it. Just follow...
13. Successful (subject) doesn't have to be difficult. Just...
14. In only 3 steps, you've just discovered...

Again, these are just ideas to get you started. Use them verbatim if you wish - or modify to suit your context or personal style. The point is, never again should you allow yourself to be stymied by any not yet written conclusion. With the above templates, there's no longer any excuse. Those will get you started. But remember to add to your collection so you'll have plenty more options to use.

Just plug in any one of these as a "plug-in" and apply it to your information. Let the words flow onto the page and you'll be amazed how fast you can do this with a little bit of experience and practice.

Write the text of your article. Then refer to these triggers to round it out with a concluding paragraph. Take any one from the list and fill in the blanks related to your topic. All you need is a sentence or two and you're finished.

Don't put it off. Get it down and get it done. Push yourself if you need to because as motivational speaker Jim Rohn said, *"We suffer one of two things: either the pain of discipline or the pain of regret. You've got to choose discipline, versus regret, because discipline weighs ounces and regret weighs tons."*

Discipline yourself to finish every article you begin because the potential payoff is unlimited and unfinished work is worse than not doing it at all.

Once you've invested even a moment into it, that's one moment you cannot get back. Complete your piece and it can only help you. But there's absolutely nothing to be gained from an incomplete article. Don't let the conclusion be a barrier when it's nothing more than a speed-bump.

Your Resource Box Is The Key To The Vault in Article Marketing

Having an effective resource box connected to every piece you create and submit is crucial to your article marketing efforts. It's the catalyst for driving traffic and reaping your just reward.

Your resource box is the one chance you have to market yourself, your product, or your web site, yet it's often neglected, under-utilized, or merely added as an afterthought.

But why go to the effort of creating quality content if you can't benefit from your work in return? That just doesn't make any sense. Yet this is exactly what happens thousands of times every single day. Solid, useful content is provided, but the author wimps out when it comes to promotion.

From the writer's perspective, the resource box (also called author's box, author's bio, etc.) is the most valuable piece of article real estate. It's the key to the vault in article marketing. Having a resource box with a link that is actively clicked is the only way you can gain a direct benefit from posting your articles anywhere other than your own site. It's the reason you take the time to craft articles and share quality content with your audience.

If your articles appeared without any connection to you, or without the opportunity to send readers to a self-serving page with a potential payoff, there would be little reason to continue sharing what you know.

You want to…

1. Make a splash with your information and…

2. Make it inviting and easy for potential customers to connect with you.

You need both elements to make article marketing work for you. Bringing customers to your business is the value the link in your resource box provides. And only by having prospects click through can you connect with them and capitalize on the entire process. In other words, to gain any measurable value, your resource box message must be seen and acted upon. The live link you place there redirects interested readers. And clicking it through is the action you want them to take.

Clicking redirects your reader's attention to your own site or blog, or an affiliate sales page where you earn commissions from every sale. That's why you do what you do. That's your article's reason for being.

If you merely share your wisdom outside, your information will surely be consumed. You might even gain a loyal following and build a reputation. But you're shooting yourself in the foot if you're not also putting an effective and enticing resource box to work for you.

Make every effort count. You've already shared your advice through your article. Readers have received a valuable payoff for the time they've invested in reading it. So you've given your time, your insight and your expertise. Now it's time to get something in return. But you need to provide the stimulus. You need to make it worthwhile. You need to make it appealing and enticing in order to make your resource box work for you.

More Tips About Winning Resource Boxes

In most cases, it's not actually a "box" with defined parameters. Instead it's up to about four or five lines of text, including a live link that's in effect, your trigger point. Your intention is to get readers to pull that trigger by clicking on the link, which brings them to your pre-selected page. Accomplish this and your article and resource box succeeds. Anything less serves no useful purpose.

Typically you're provided with 450 characters - which is roughly one paragraph of space. The first line of this paragraph is about 85 characters in length. So approximately four and a half lines like that one is what you have to play with.

In some cases, you're given much more space. For example, ezinearticles.com now allows up to 300 words in your resource box. But I suggest a "less is more" strategy be put into place.

You want to tease and tempt readers to click through your link, where you can connect with them and build a relationship, or instigate the sales process right away.

If you write a 300-word article and include a 300-word resource box, it's hard to imagine it not sounding overly commercial. Not exactly the kind of vibe you want to project. You're better off delivering quality content and then enticing your reader to get more of what they want by connecting to the source of the information they just enjoyed.

You don't need to sell them on your product or membership site. Nor should you give them the entire history of your business. Instead, promise more of what they want… more of the value they received.

Make them an irresistible offer, one that can only be had by clicking through. Arouse their curiosity by suggesting that there's much more to the story than what you just revealed in your article. Promise the path to get more of the helpful information they seek. And this can always be done with just a single powerful paragraph.

Here's an article marketing formula that works every time:

1. Capture the ATTENTION of your target audience (TITLE)

2. Deliver quality, unique content (BODY COPY)

3. Give readers a COMPELLING REASON to click on your link with an alluring OFFER and a CALL TO ACTION (Resource Box)

Once your readers arrive at your site you can capture their email addresses and get them into your marketing funnel. That's probably the best long-term value strategy.

But you can also begin selling to them directly or by making other offers available through affiliate links, banner ads, or Adsense advertising on your site. In order to get true prospects there from your article marketing means you must first provide useful, valuable content and then promise something more.

The Most Important Element of a Successful Resource Box

It's the offer or promise that makes or breaks your resource box.

Think about it. Your title captured attention and your content delivered value. So your reader kept on reading. Making it through the text qualifies readers as genuine prospects for your congruent product, business, or affiliate offer.

If visitors weren't true prospects, they would have lost interest at some point and already fled to greener pastures elsewhere.

Now that your readers have completed the text, it's up to your resource box to reel them in and the best way to do that is to give them more of the same or better and offer it for free.

To maximize your return from this strategy, make redeeming your free offer, contingent upon signing up to your mailing list. This means readers will have to leave their email address in the form on your web site to cash in on your free offer. For most who are hungry for the kind of special information you provide, that shouldn't be too much of an issue.

You don't have to do it this way, but it's exactly what most top marketers do. Quality, on-target, solution-oriented and original information is what readers value most. They don't want a rehash of the commonplace information that abounds online. How you serve up that free information is really up to you. There are lots of ways. For example, you could...

Compile several of your best articles into an ebook
Write a special report
Create an ebook
Provide a subscription to your newsletter
Offer a downloadable audio MP3
Interview another exert and offer the recording and/or transcript
Develop an e-course and deliver it via several emails over time
Create a series of video tutorials

Just like the articles you provide, your free offer needs to serve up original, quality content that your target niche wants. Any method can work well. Choose the one that best suits your audience and can be accomplished with your existing resources. In other words, don't go out and buy an expensive video camera or software program right away just to create a video product as a giveaway. If you don't already have those tools, it would be smarter to use a format that you already have the capability and resources to create.

Make whatever you offer of significant benefit to your target prospect. Create it as unique, exclusive content that can only be obtained one way. You need to create information that is in fact helpful and you need to promote it as such in your resource box. You can have the most amazing, information-loaded free report ever created as your lure, but if you fail to "sell" readers on snagging it for themselves, it doesn't mean squat.

Decide on a free offer that can be used in any resource box your niche market might see. Whatever you promise needs to be a good match for the audience. So if your market is "dog training" in general, your free offer should serve owners of all breeds. Make it suitable to only a narrow portion of your potential viewing audience and you limit the pulling power of the offer.

You want your offer to be applicable to any article that you write for that particular niche and there's nothing stopping you from creating more than one freebie. But if you want to attain maximum leverage from your efforts, naturally you'll want to make your primary offer something that appeals specifically to the kind of prospects you want to attract.

It's your article that first captured their attention. Never forget that. Connect the topic of your article to your offer. In other words, position the offer as a more detailed and complete solution. The article starts the process and the free offer takes it to the next level.

It's a good idea to create and save several different versions of your resource box. Then take the one that's the best fit and customize it slightly to merge smoothly with the article just completed. Speak the same language of your article and in particular, the title you've selected. You could even shape your resource box to be your actual conclusion, or a part thereof. Feature the same keyword term once in your resource box and turn it into anchor text that links back to whatever page you want to send prospects to.

More Resource Box Strategies To Make Your Article Writing Pay Off in Spades

Make every word count. Don't add extra copy just because you have the space available. The second your prospect's interest fades is the second she vanishes into the vast online universe, likely to never return again. Think of the resource box as a small classified ad.

In one paragraph of text you've got to:

- Capture your prospect's ATTENTION…

- Fan the spark of INTEREST into an intense flame…
- Present an IRRESISTIBLE OFFER that can be obtained instantly and at no cost… and…
- Guide your prospect to take SPECIFIC ACTION by clicking your link to collect on your big promise.

Make the resource box the next natural and logical step for the prospect. You've grabbed attention and interest and delivered quality content. Your reader is feeling good about what she just discovered. At the same time, a positive impression of you, the provider of said information forms in the reader's mind.

But what can you do about it?

Seize the opportunity at once. Take full advantage of the warm, fuzzy feelings generated as a result of your content and inspire your reader to take the action you want her to take. That means clicking on your link in search of more relevant information.

In a classified ad, every word counts. The same holds true for the article resource box. Make it as powerful and as lean as you can and still make sense. But you should avoid the abbreviations that are often used in small classified ads to conserve space and cut costs. Resource box space allowances aren't quite so tight. So be sure to use complete sentences and full words. Make it alluring and clear.

Rather than setting your resource box apart, make it blend smoothly with your article. Ezinearticles.com facilitates this process beautifully. Rather than creating a separate author's box which takes the eye away from the main text, the resource box merges right into the article. It uses the same font and the same text size, with no divisive lines separating the content from the promotional paragraph. This helps facilitate the "natural next step" approach that works so well in article marketing.

Make Your Resource Box Offer the Perfect Fit

Feed off the content of your article. Build on the interest it creates. Connect your resource box to the content just delivered in a way that leads readers in the direction you want them to go. Let your resource box pave the way to the next step for prospects.

Never assume that reading (and taking action on) the message delivered in your resource box is a given. You've got to make it appealing... alluring... inviting... and exciting. Think of your content as a headline. Your reader has just processed the material in your article. But now she's arrived at a fork in the road as the content portion winds down.

Should she go this way or that? That's where your resource box needs to figuratively leap off the page and make that decision an easy one.

You've just delivered value to your prospect. But to get any value in return, you have to win over your reader and get her to visit. In most cases, this means clicking on your live link.

But some directories, blogs and newsletters that pick up your article won't allow live links in the resource box. If that's the case, it means copying and pasting, or manually entering your URL in the search field of your user's browser. To get anyone to do that, especially those used to the ease and speed of online travel by clicking, means you've got to grab them by the eyeballs and pull them in with an irresistible promise or offer.

Lead prospects to what it is they want. This can often mean leveraging the interest generated from your article to move them one step further along in the process. And it's the most critical step for you because without it, you lose.

Keep in mind however, that only a percentage of readers who visit your article will ever click on your link. That's just the way it is. But your task is to maximize the rate at which they click through (also known as the conversion rate). You want to turn readers into prospects and the way to do it is to get as many of them as possible to follow your directive.

Studies indicate that the lion's share of online traffic is primarily searching for information. It was the information contained in your article is the secret because that's what first captured the searcher's attention. If the article proved to be a good match to the information they desired, your link stands out like a bright beacon against a blackened sky. But if it misses the mark - your link becomes invisible and irrelevant.

Delivering quality information sets you up to achieve a successful outcome. Your intention is to lead readers to your site in a natural progression. Deliver what they want. Then lure them inside with the promise of even more high-value information. In order to get, you have to first give. That's just the way the universe seems to work.

Articles are the starting point. Targeted articles attract the right kind of prospects when the content fits what the information seeker wants. Readers are drawn to the content as promised in the title. Make your resource box compatible with those desires and you'll increase the number of prospects introduced to your business.

12 Powerful and Profitable Resource Box Tips

Remember that your resource box is the connecting link between you and your potential customers. Here, in summary form, are 12 powerful and profitable tips to help you attract more traffic from every article you write:

1. Make an impact. You only have one shot at making a positive first impression. Your resource box gives you one chance to "wow" readers and pull them into your marketing funnel. Avoid the meager results a ho-hum resource box delivers by knowing what your prospects want and then promising a big benefit. Make it easy and irresistible to respond by offering something of value at no cost.

2. Develop an offer that's an ideal match to those people who read your article. What's in it for the reader to click on your link and visit your site? It's all about the offer. Give them something no one else does. Make your gift item something that's not just unique but exclusive. When yours is the only door leading to paradise, it's going to get opened more than one that promises the same thing as other people do. To get more clicks, make your offer more valuable and appealing to the specific audience you want to serve.

3. Condense your resource box copy to one powerful paragraph. Keep it short and to the point. Shorter is better than longer to entice prospects. Grab attention with a headline that speaks directly to your prospect. Than present an offer that's too tempting to pass by.

4. Provide a single direction. That means giving your reader a single link to click on. This is not the place to list all of your web sites. Just lead them to the one page that provides the most compatible match.

5. Include a line of biographical information about the author ONLY if it makes sense to do so. Add a relevant achievement that qualifies you to speak on the topic. For example, if your article and site is about parachuting, it makes sense to tell your audience that you're a veteran of 73 jumps in 5 different countries. It's not about bragging, it's about relevancy and positioning.

6. Use both your first and last name. Every article is another way for people to discover you and what you offer. Begin building a reputation with the next article you craft. Everything you write after that just adds wood to the fire. Perception is everything. Don't miss out on an opportunity to remind people about what you do. You can always use different pen names with different niches. This will help keep others who see your success in one niche from becoming your competitor in another.

7. Tell readers what to do. I'm not for a moment suggesting that you become obnoxious – quite the contrary. But you do need to lead people to your particular solution. If you simply place it on the table before them, some will reach for it and some won't. You want maximum value so tell people what to do next. Provide a clear call to action. Here's an example – "Click here now to claim your free copy of my 29-page report, - How to double your sales in half the time".

8. Edit your resource box for clarity and power. Read it out loud. If you trip over your words, fix them. If you stumble a little, be sure smooth over any rough spots. And be sure to check and double check your link to make sure it's 100% accurate. One slight mishap could cost you thousands of new prospects. Always be sure your link is live and working perfectly.

9. Think of your resource box as an "elevator speech"… a ten second sound bite… or as a quick introduction to you and your business. There's no time or space for a warm-up or wandering thought. Hit hard and hit fast. Deliver a headline that grabs eyeballs, an offer that pulls like a magnet, and the means to collect on the promise and thereby get something more that interested prospects will love.

10. Feature the main keyword combination used in the article and make it a live link that connects to your site. Links are recognized by the search engines. When the same keyword phrase is also sprinkled throughout the text, the combination tends to give you greater relevancy and therefore, exposure.

11. Use keyboard artwork (~*|->>) sparingly to add eye-appeal to any text-only message. With a resource box, the only tools at your disposal are your words and the link to your site. Whatever words you choose need to temporarily engage prospects and stimulate their natural desire. But you can also inject an element of design into your resource box by the clever (and restrained) use of symbols created by keystrokes. One effective way is the use of arrows pointing to your URL like this: == >> http://refdesk.com

12. Inject a little curiosity and you'll inspire hoards of readers to click your link. For example... following an article that offers "Quick tips for faster article writing", I might use this as my resource box copy...

"Are you making the same costly mistakes 9 out 10 article writers do? Slash your article writing time in half and produce high quality content at the same time with my free report '7 Time-Wasting Traps Most Article Writers Fall Into & How To Avoid Them Completely'. Click here for your FREE 10-page report: ->> website listed here"

How To Crank Out Quality, Unique Articles Fast With Simple "Plug 'n Play" Templates

When asked by a client about the fastest way to repeatedly write decent articles, this essentially was my reply: Anyone can learn how to write articles quickly and it's a great way to create fresh content regularly that you can post on your own web site or blog.

If you're already an article marketer, or you plan on becoming one - learning how to write at hyper-speed can make all the difference. This method can also be applied to writing content for others. The faster you can write them, the more money you'll make from your article writing service.

Please don't confuse these quick and efficient article writing tips with creating weak content - just to get something out there. My position is that quality information of value needs to be your first priority. So you should always approach your article writing in a helpful spirit, to provide genuine value to those who take the time to read your content.

Begin With Keywords

Keywords are a great place to start if you want to gain any benefit from the search engines. If you don't already have a large list of potential keywords, get one by using the free Google keyword tool. If you've got a few hundred keyword terms – it's easy to get off to a flying start. If you've got more, that's great too. But if you've only got a few, you should consider adding to your list before you kick this method into high gear.

Having a long list gives you multiple options. As you scan your printed page of keywords, certain terms will seem easier to write about than others. Another thing that tends to happen is this: your creativity starts to flourish. Certain terms trigger automatic associations. Place a small check-mark next to any term that catches your attention, as you continue making your way through the list.

By the time you complete the list, you may have a dozen or more marked keyword terms. I'm all for keeping things as simple as can be, so I encourage you to start with one of these keywords.

Plug In a Title

Next, refer to the title templates provided and fit your chosen keyword term inside. Quick article writing is made possible with the right kind of title.

To help you get a better picture, let's use "car detailing" as our niche and "car detailing tips" as our first keyword. With this particular keyword term, you've got an easy foundation from which to construct an article. Not all keywords are this juicy and ripe for the picking.

To maximize the value of keywords, it's important to place them at the very beginning of your title whenever possible. So we take our "car detailing tips" and we scan through the more than 700 title templates, looking for something that might make a good fit. Here are a few...

- Car Detailing Tips: Breakthroughs That Can Transform Any Well-Used Car into Showroom-Like Condition
- Car Detailing Tips For Beginners
- Dirt-Cheap Car Detailing Tips Every Do-It-Yourselfer Needs To Know

With your keyword term selected, all you need to do is scan the list of "idea-starters". In just minutes, you could easily have multiple article titles (and topics) from just one keyword phrase.

Flesh-Out Your Content

Your title points you in the right direction. But you still need to build the content to support it. Remember that one super-easy technique is to "think in threes". So with each article you write, you need three main support points. You can include more of course, but three will often give you enough to write to write about in one article.

Think of the first three things that come mind as your read your title. Go with whatever associations come to mind. Taking an example above – "Car Detailing Tips For Beginners" - three terms I can easily associate with the topic are - *Car Detailing Tools, Work Environment* and *Green Cleaning Solutions.* Your associations would likely be different from mine and that's a good thing. With just a title and three supporting ideas – I've got the outline of an article created in very little time.

If the associations don't flow quickly and easily, or you simply want to take a different approach, refer to your list of "content idea triggers" as a guide. For example, think of three frequently asked questions, three key ideas, three common problems, or three preventable mistakes people make when doing their own car detailing and you've got the framework for another article in just seconds.

One More Thing Before You Start Writing

As mentioned, it's important to have a few different resource boxes ready to go, so all you have to do is copy and paste them into your article. If you wait until after you write your article, it's easy to get tripped up at the resource box phase. This is easy to see and understand because where the article ends and the resource box begins, represents a significant shift in your writing. For search engine optimization, carefully select the keywords you want to use as anchor text.

In article writing, you're share information with your readers. It's pure content. Resource boxes on the other hand, are essentially marketing materials, designed to lead the reader directly to your site.

In what is typically a small amount of space, you've got to lure as many prospects as possible, with something of obvious interest. The mission of your resource box is to direct readers to click on your link as their next, most immediate course of action. It's the only way you can benefit from the whole process of sharing information with an audience.

What's the easiest way to create a compelling resource box that attracts the kind of prospects you want to attract? Answer: Model other successful resource boxes. Again, having a collection of resource boxes to kick-start your own can only help.

Start Writing

At this point you're ready to begin the writing phase of article creation. You've got your keyword term, title, outline and resource box. Now it's just a matter of turning what you've got into an interesting and informative piece of content.

Not sure how to launch into your article? For many new article writers, the one big stumbling block is the introduction. Once they get that first half-sentence written, they're on their way.

Of course, it's no problem at all when you have a list of lead templates at your disposal. You might also want to check out the rest of this site for additional article writing tips.

To continue with our "car detailing" example, we need an opening sentence to start the engine running. Here are some possibilities that only took a few seconds:

- Are you frustrated by the high price of car detailing services, when you can do a better job yourself at home?
- Could this be the one stumbling block to getting professional results from your own, do-it-yourself car detailing?
- In this article, I'm going to let you in the 3 car detailing tips the pros hope you never discover on your own.

To complete the body copy of your article, simple refer to your three main ideas. Now take these points or supporting ideas and write a paragraph of two on each. You haven't got time to waste, so simply take one of these ideas at a time and write whatever comes to mind that pertains to your article title. This is important in producing a quality article and having it all tie together nicely.

If you encounter a roadblock don't panic. Instead, take your supporting idea and break it down into three parts by identifying three words that you associate to this idea or term. This system is totally flexible, so just go where your mind takes you - as long as it's related to your main topic in some way.

Another approach to near-instant content creation is to use action words as thought triggers. Using the keyword term "green cleaning solutions" - you scan the list of action words and grab those that capture your interest. Accomplish, Address, Assault, and Assure jump out at me right away. I've only looked at verbs beginning with "A" so far, but you can surely see how this approach will help you create quality and original articles swiftly.

If you want to include a conclusion to your article, once again, there's no need to struggle or cause any unnecessary delays in your writing productivity. Peruse your list of conclusion templates and grab one that works for you. All you need is the spark and that's what article writing templates give you.

Top Ten Time-Saving Tips For Article Writers

When it comes to effective article writing, it pays to write with your reader in mind. This means creating useful content. But you've also got to work at an efficient pace, or it will be too easy to avoid writing more articles in the future. Below are 10 time-saving tips for article writers.

1. Plan your article and then write it. The process of article creation involves thinking, planning, typing or speaking. Map out your article in advance. Think of the key points, you want to include and keep it simple. When you sit down to create your article, simply describe each of the key points as quickly as you can. As your concept develops in your mind, capture it on the page. That's the essence of article writing. Don't judge your writing until your piece is complete. Get it done. Then work to improve it. Planning first and then writing your articles utilizes both halves of your brain the way nature intended.

2. Tap into your inner genius. Speed-writing forces your mind to get to the good stuff without delay. You have an idea that you would like to convey in your article, and you want to do so effectively and efficiently. When you write it fast you tap into the essence of the concept, letting your creativity spill onto the page. Write it at a rapid speed and you'll often astound yourself with the quality of material your mind generates. When you write slowly, you stifle your natural creativity. When you analyze and assess as you write, you make productive writing impossible. Write it first, polish it after.

3. Set your target and make a commitment. We're all busy. But what happens is the days, weeks, months, and years slip by and sometimes we miss out on achieving the things we resolved to achieve at the start of the year. But a successful year begins with a successful day and that's one that moves you closer to your objective. Decide how many articles you're going to write on your specific niche and make it happen. The only problem you'll ever have in getting it done is you. Don't let anything (including yourself) get in your way and the results you want will have to be yours if you persist.

4. Set aside enough time every day to reach your daily objectives. Fast article writing involves time management. Even at supersonic writing speeds, there's still time involved in writing each piece. If you don't manage your time, you're setting up unnecessary blocks that will only impede your progress.

5. List several article titles before beginning your writing session. Highly-productive article writing requires grouping several articles together and working on them concurrently. Make your goal of multiple articles attainable by creating the titles first. List 10 article topics in advance and you're on the way to having them all completed. When your mind can visualize multiple sub-topics, you break through any resistance. Truth is… you are capable of much more than you probably imagine and you have plenty of unique, in-demand article ideas inside, just waiting to be unleashed.

6. Write often. There's a myth that writing is hard. But it's not actually. Thinking (or worrying) about it is much harder on you than actually sitting down and rolling up your sleeves. Writing is communication and effective writing is effective communication. Putting your thoughts and ideas into words that are instantly clear is what it's all about and the more you do it, the more it becomes a natural form of expression for you.

7. Simplify the complex. Explain things in a way that any reader can grasp. Use words that are easily understood. Make your article easy to read at a fast pace. What is it that you enjoy about good reading? When you enjoy your reading, one of the big reasons typically is that the book is well written. It's simple… concise… clear… and maybe even clever. But it draws you in and you move through it fast. It feels like the writer created it effortlessly. Communicate the same way in your articles.

8. Make article writing part of your routine. You can find time to write more articles - everyone can. If you really want to, you can squeeze in an extra 15 to 30 minutes a day, even with a jam-packed schedule. All you have to do is make it a priority. Look for opportunities to grab a few minutes here and there. Keep a notepad with you and use found time to generate new article ideas and outlines.

9. Engage your inner power. Article writing involves both sides of your brain. The left brain is the logical side. Use it to outline your content and to edit later. The right brain is the creative and freewheeling part that's used to express your thoughts, ideas and images into sentences and paragraphs. The right side is about getting your ideas onto paper in a coherent manner. Both sides of the brain are important to writing quality articles fast. If you can use both in harmony your writing will be efficient and organized. But when logic interrupts the creative flow, or when creativity goes off the rails, writing productivity and the clarity of your communication suffers.

10. "Speak" your articles. Your mind works faster than your fingers – that's just the way it is. You can think faster than you can type. No one has fingers that can move across the keyboard as fast as they can form thoughts in their mind. Therefore your most productive article writing process involves a more direct expression of your thoughts. This is best achieved through your own voice when you speak your articles into a recording device or software, rather than write them in the traditional way.

Another Ten Time-Saving Tips For Article Writers

1. Channel your creativity. Your mind is a powerhouse of creative ideas and inspiration. Use it effectively and it becomes a perpetual article topic generator. Writing articles is simply a matter of tapping into your vast mental storehouse and allowing your mind to generate ideas. Then you harness those ideas and shape them into individual articles. As you allow it to do its work, your mind will spit out more interesting ideas on related topics - on demand. Write them down as they come. Then it's just a matter of generating associated ideas and clearly communicating your message to the reader.

2. Free yourself. Write when you should be writing and ignore everything else, including your inner critic. Leave the editing as the last step in the process. Fix it only after you have written it. If you don't allow yourself unlimited freedom to simply communicate, you won't get your article completed as quickly as you could. You have to let yourself go to write most effectively.

3. Take action to overcome inertia. You can beat procrastination by getting started now. What have you got to fear? If you want to write an article, just do it. State your idea and then shape it into a title that includes your main keyword term. Then list the first 3 to 7 ideas related to that subject that come to mind. That's enough to get you going. Now that you have the framework, write the article. You'll be done before you know it.

4. Map out each article individually. Follow the simple method above for any article and you'll quickly be on your way. Creating a simple framework or plan in advance makes the writing easy by focusing your efforts in a productive way. Writing is only challenging when you're stuck wondering which way to go. Even the most basic framework allows you to go with the flow rather than fight against the current.

5. Keep your writing light and make it fun. If it's fun, you'll look forward to writing more. If it's painful, you'll avoid it at all costs. That's why it helps to specialize in a niche that you're passionate about.

6. Start with an easy topic. Some will be obvious, others less so. Starting with an easy article topic gives you momentum and energy which will help you tackle the more challenging topics. When your potential topic is more challenging to you, list it as a preliminary step at the top of a blank sheet of paper. Next, start with a vague notion about what you want to write and think of descriptive words that relate to your sub-topic and shape these associated words into a simple article outline. A basic outline of only a few words is often enough to create a strong article in just minutes.

7. Turn your ideas into assets. Creating an article (which in turn becomes an asset) is about taking the rough idea from your outline and shaping it into sentences and paragraphs. Your outline focuses your attention. It gives you a specific direction. Transferring your raw idea into asset form means putting your outline into action by explaining your key points logically with sentences readers can easily read and understand.

8. Keep the article speed-writing formula before you until it's locked into your memory. This system enables you to create your own original pieces on demand. Start with the title and a few significant words or statements and then tailor these details into a complete article. It's easiest when you refer to the templates and simply plug them in. This kick-starts your brain and triggers your natural creativity.

9. Repeat the process again and again. "Repetition is the mother of skill" says human potential giant, Tony Robbins. Make article writing part of your daily routine and you'll continue to write better articles in less time. The more you apply these ideas, the easier it gets and the more effective they become. Your confidence soars as you continue to put these shortcuts to work for you, helping you create more articles in less time.

10. Act fast to capture your ideas. Article speed-writing is about shaping your concepts into meaningful descriptions as quickly as possible. Turn trigger points into content. Whatever comes to mind as you write, get it down. Write as fast as you can, and you tap into that stream of nonstop ideas your mind turns over to you whenever you engage it.

3 Ways To Write Articles For Fun and Profit

Articles can make or break your online business. Most top marketers write articles (or have them written for them) on a regular basis to constantly attract a steady stream of fresh, new prospects. Articles represent content and as such, are a way to "pre-sell" any product, service or business.

Everyone online should be using articles to build their businesses and grow their incomes. But there's one huge stumbling block that stands in the way and that is - How can make profitable article writing and fun and productive exercise?

Let me share three simple techniques to make this happen.

Method #1: Make a List

If you can write a grocery list, you can use this simple technique to create a helpful and informative article in minutes. Just take the topic you're writing about and provide a method and sequence.

For example, if your article was about writing articles, you would simply list the steps involved. Use numbers or bullet points to separate each step in the system.

1. Create a list of keywords.

2. Use Title Templates to turn those keywords into titles.
3. List 3 important details you want to share about the subject.
4. Write it up in sentences and paragraphs.
5. Add an introduction and possibly a conclusion as well.
6. Attach your resource box to the article.

To flesh out your article, write a sentence or two about each point. What words do you associate to each key point or supporting idea? Write down the first 3 significant terms that come to mind. Then use these associated words to build your content. Do this for each of your main points and you've written your article.

Method #2: Share a Personal Experience

This method is very effective because you're telling it like nobody else can. It's your personal experience and perspective that makes your article unique.

Deliver the information you uncovered by actually going through the experience. Start at the beginning and cover each of the important elements. Tell your story and you've got content that is certain to be 100% original.

Method #3: Teach a Mini-Lesson

Imagine that you're at the front of the room teaching a bunch of adults enrolled in a continuing education program. The subject of your class is the subject of your article.

How can you teach someone else what you know in a way that they're sure to understand? Think back to the best teacher you ever had and recall what made this individual a personal favourite of yours. Then simply pretend that YOU are this special teacher.

But remember, you've only got a few short minutes to convey your information on the topic. So you need an overview to follow. Then knock off one point at a time and illustrate it in a way that makes sense. There you have it - 3 simple ways to write articles easily.

Article Writing Made Easier

Article writing can be a gruelling task, or a simple and straightforward one. Anyone can write an article. But for most first-timers, it's a tedious, brain-draining exercise. It's this way only because these new writers lack a basic writing system. Once they learn to simplify the process, article writing is far less challenging and time consuming than it was.

Some would have you think that writing articles is something best left to the experienced professionals. Well, you could outsource all the articles you want if you've got an unlimited budget. But even that's not as easy as it seems as you'll spend tons of time sourcing article writers and micro-managing them and checking their work.

Article writing is actually such a simple process once you figure it out, that I recommend it to every online marketer, entrepreneur and business. Successful article writing takes just three things in minimal quantity: time, effort, and a simple system.

Just decide to do it and you're halfway home. With practice, you can write a quality article in minutes instead of hours. You'll have to focus your efforts and you need a simple and reliable system to pull this off.

Articles are a great way to market with content and to draw prospects and customers to your site. The basic process of writing a quality article is something anyone can learn and master. It probably won't happen overnight... but it need not take months either.

The first step is to select a topic related to your business. Think about what your prospects and customers would like to know. What details could you share that would provide VALUE to those in your marketplace?

Gather your raw information. Write from your experience and then add extra material as needed after doing your research.

Think about what your average customer knows and probably doesn't know. What interesting and helpful little-known facts can you deliver?

Figure out your angle. Articles are short pieces, so you need to choose one specific idea or element for each article. Think about the information you already possess. What new information have you uncovered that would be interesting to others?

Your angle is conveyed in the title. Think in terms of "How To" or "3 Ways To" and then just fill in the rest in a compelling way. Then think of the first 3 -7 points that come to mind as you ponder your title and jot them down. You now have a title and the main points of your article.

All you need now is to write a paragraph or two on each point while adding an introduction and conclusion. That's the basic framework of an article. Your introduction should feed off your title and then set the stage for the rest of the article. Your conclusion should first and foremost, lead readers straight to your web site.

Random Tips, Tactics and Reminders for Writing Quality Articles Fast

Strategy

Choose your overall market niches carefully. If you want to make writing hundreds of articles manageable, choose something you're passionate about. If you're a dog lover, writing articles about dogs, dog food, dog training and so on is easy. But if your general topic isn't something you're into, it will eventually feel like you're rowing upstream. When you're pumped up about sharing information, it's easy to get into a rhythm where your write article after article and share top quality material. When you're enthusiastic about your topic, it's amazing how fast those articles materialize.

Get enthusiastic about the information you're sharing. Enthusiasm energizes your writing. This means you'll write better content in less time. When you raise your level of enthusiasm - each step in the process becomes easier. You'll sail through your article writing and feel great about your accomplishments and your audience will value it more.

Transfer your ideas to the page. Effective article writing means communicating your thoughts, ideas and vision with the written word with clarity and understanding. Step one is to decide what it is you want to communicate. In other words, determine the main idea and the key points related to that main idea. Then explain it as though you were describing something you're passionate about to a friend. Capture your verbal delivery and you've got the makings of another quality article.

Know what you want out of each article before you write it. If your main objective is to convey expertise, you would probably opt for a longer, more detailed article. If instead you're article is one of a number of lead-generators to place in various article directories, it might be best to write short, concise articles. Both types of articles can serve you, but each has a different purpose. Whatever the method, strive to convey quality information in a way that's easy for your readers to grasp.

Focus on your article topic from the start. Decide on the subject and your key points and you'll be setting yourself up to write your article faster. Instantly, you'll have a starting point and your overall scope defined, so meandering doesn't occur. Your planning provides a guaranteed roadmap that will take you straight to your destination of choice.

List the easy subjects first. When considering a new article topic, build a list of possible approaches. Jot down whatever comes to mind. It could be "Three secrets of...", "Where most people go wrong with...", or "7 simple steps to...". Anything at all is applicable here. Use the templates provided in this course and there will be no stopping you. Just get a bunch of possible angles listed. Then scan the page and pick the one approach that leaps out as an obvious choice. That's your starting point. Take that and craft an outline. Then peruse your list once again and look for more low-hanging fruit. Grab hold of whatever appeals to you in the moment and shape it into an outline for you can use.

Stay on track. Keep your intention in mind as you write each piece. Set out to deliver quality information so the reader will want more. Make your points clear and meaningful and you give yourself the best chance of getting more readers to click. Build your reputation with solid content. Build your business by directing readers back to your web site, blog, squeeze page, or sales page.

Experiment first and then use the approach that works best for you. One-word topics can be a help or a hindrance - depending on specifics and your state of mind at the time. With one word as your subject, the sky's the limit as to how you approach it. But unlimited possibility can also create mental blocks. It's like having unlimited brands of a single item to choose from at the grocery store. Making a selection can be a challenge. When that's the case, take your one-word subject and expand it into a sentence. This gives you a more specific direction. It channels your broad topic into something more manageable. Write the essence of an idea in one line and capture any supporting details that arise.

Use your imagination. Tell it as only you can. Be unique. Demonstrate your point with metaphors, analogies, stories, or examples. How can you best communicate this core idea? Adapt your plan to your ideas, background, stories and style. Write from the heart and from personal experience.

Teach your reader something new. As you write, think of yourself as a teacher or trainer. You have an idea to get across – that's your purpose. Consider this: What's the most effective way to teach your lesson? How can you communicate your core concept in a way that your reader is sure to get it? Think of the best teacher, trainer or seminar leader you ever experienced. How would they communicate this concept or method? Think like a teacher and explain your points in a way that's easily and instantly understood.

Become a leader or guide. Think of each article as a path the reader needs to take. Lead your prospect to action and you'll both get the desired result. Your ultimate intention is to get them to click the link in your resource box. But they won't do that unless they first find value in your information. Every sentence and paragraph either encourages further readership, or it steers those readers in another direction. Every sentence has to make the reader want to continue reading. If your information falls short and the reader flees, your efforts in writing the article will be lost on that prospect forever.

Seek and find. Look at your lists of key points for each article you've written. What's missing? Look for any elements that you might have overlooked. These little nuggets can provide additional article content and value.

Go with the flow. Magic happens when you sail along, making one point after another. There's no better feeling than tapping into your own creative expression and letting it carry you on to completion. When you enter into "stream of consciousness" writing, the words flow effortlessly and your productivity soars.

Don't stop to read what you've written.

Writing is first and foremost about letting your ideas pour onto the page. Get it done and then move onto the next article. After you've written a bunch, then go back and polish them up. If you interrupt your writing to re-read, analyze, or criticize your work, you shut down your creative machinery. It's like you're operating on one cylinder when you're designed to be a finely-tuned, twelve-cylinder powerhouse.

Keep a separate notebook nearby to capture extra ideas. I use a small note pad tucked into my pocket calendar. When you're deeply engaged in writing articles, other breakthrough ideas can come to you in a flash. Capture ideas before they escape. Then get back on track. If you ignore these flashes of insight, you'll lose out on some of your brightest and shiniest gems. Careful though. If you spend more than a brief moment, it's easy to lose your writing momentum.

Divide your article writing activities up into segments. If, for example, you choose to create ten articles at a time, do them in a productive way. Establish your ten topics. Then map out each article. Provide just enough detail to steer you on the right path - one that's in alignment with each one of your titles. Then group your writing together. Write one article and then move onto the next. Focus for a few moments on your new outline and lock the core idea into your mind. Set your timer and start writing. Breaking up your tasks this way allows you to work more efficiently.

Choose a single angle as you flesh your article out. You could potentially proceed in a hundred different directions and add multiple articles from the same basic content. And that may be something you'll want to do that later. It's best to expand your idea in just one direction. Add supporting words, concepts and insights -- and keep it brief. Make your supporting information specific and related to your topic.

Simple is best. It's only one article you're dealing with at the moment, so it need not take much time to create a simple structure. Then go back and tap into your unlimited mind some more. Start with the most obvious ideas first and build a list of topics and/or titles. Capture the most worthy ideas pertaining to each topic, title, or keyword and quickly sketch out a framework. Every single topic can be spun in numerous ways. Every keyword term in your mind can spark dozens more. The point is to channel your creativity to create article content quickly.

Take a moment to get focused before you write. Look over your outline, harness your thinking and then start writing. Let your supporting ideas pour from your mind to the page as quickly as they appear. Stay in step with your outline and you'll remain on course with the core idea you want to express.

Think of each article as a mini-lesson, rather than a complete course. You introduce your topic, mention 3-7 supporting points and then you quickly review the essence of what you've covered by summing it up for the reader. "How to" articles, numbered lists of tips (example: 5 Simples Steps To) and instructional guides all make for great articles. Another way to create stellar content is to reveal common mistakes or myths associated with your topic.

Present your information in a logical sequence. Make the details make sense to the reader. Start at the beginning and work your way through to the end. If it's a random list with no obvious pattern, start and end your list with your most valuable or dramatic points. Starting strong ensures that your reader is pulled inside. Finishing with equal impact leaves a positive impression and makes getting the click to your money page much more likely.

Divide lengthy content into multiple pieces. While it usually pays off to have longer articles on your own site, when posting to article directories, it can sometimes pay to break up your content.

If your article topic involves a lengthy list of points, consider splitting it into a couple of smaller articles. As long as you're providing original information of value, you should be fine. But don't make your articles too short. All you need is three points to craft a decent article. You could choose a greater quantity, like "Seven Sure-Fire Strategies..." if you like. But if your list of key points turns your article into a 1600-word creation or longer – it's best to split it up.

Speaking of lists, they're a great way to deliver information. Numbered lists form the basis of popular articles in directories, search engine results, and on high-traffic web sites such as Digg. They're also surprisingly easy to write. If you can shape your content around a numbered list of anywhere from 3-10 items, it's a proven approach that often attracts a higher readership by default.

Conclude your articles on a strong note. Go out with a bang instead of a whimper. When someone reads through your article in its entirety, they're obviously interested in the subject at hand. But it's usually the last sentence or paragraph your reader consumes before making an instantaneous decision about clicking through or clicking away. The end of your article is a definite turning point that can be the difference between success and failure. Give readers something they can feel good about you stand a better chance of getting the click.

Improve your writing system and boost your productivity as you go. The first time you try to write an article in fifteen minutes, you might think it's difficult, if not impossible. But instead of doubting your capability, give it your best shot. If you fail to meet the deadline the first time, that's okay. After all, you've never attempted it before. Start again. But this time, pay attention to the deadline and get your details down quickly. Force yourself to stick to the deadline. When you can repeatedly write an article in 15 minutes, shorten the allowable time to twelve minutes. Continue this process by reducing the time allowed until you reach your optimum productivity range.

By pushing yourself and simplifying your system as you go, you'll discover that it's possible to write quality articles even faster. Setting a deadline and using a timer to enforce it triggers high-output action.

Repeat the article writing process over and over again – that's how you develop proficiency in anything. Adapt the system to suite your style and make it your own. Write multiple articles in each writing session and do this as frequently as you ca. If you write articles faster and faster, you'll continually set new speed standards for yourself. Anything less at this point won't sit well with you because you've stretched your mind and skill to a new level. Repetitive speed writing will improve your written word communications.

Planning

Determine your theme in advance. Each article should have a central idea - an idea that is revealed in the title. When you have a working title, you understand immediately the kind of content your article needs to contain. At the core of every article, is one basic concept or idea and you need to be clear on what that idea is before you begin writing.

Map out your concept in advance. You could potentially proceed in a hundred different directions from the same basic content. That's why you should choose a specific path early on. Planning can be done in seconds and it will spare you inevitable frustration later. Start with a keyword, topic, or potential title. Capture it by jotting it down. That's important. You need to seize the concept or idea you want to share before it escapes you. What first comes to mind when you think about your proposed topic or when you read the title? Get it down on paper (or on your computer) and use it as your launch pad.

Divide the topic into chunks. Breaking it down into pieces makes the writing easy. Start by estimating the total size of your article. How long will your introduction be? What about a conclusion? How many points will you include? Break it down and what seems like a large and difficult task becomes easily manageable.

Emphasize your core message. When mapping out your article, identify the BIG idea you want to discuss and ensure that every supporting idea relates to this core concept. If you begin writing your article without first mapping and determining its scope, you'll fizzle out. You might start off with a bang, but eventually you'll hit a dead end or you'll drift off in a different direction.

Stay true to your main message. It's vital that you do so.

Flesh out your article by building a list. Simply jot down a title and list the key points you want to cover. If it's a "how to" article, briefly list each step involved. If it's a "numbered list" article, indicate each point on the list as succinctly as possible.

Then all you have to do is write it.

Shape the content into sentences and paragraphs with creative elaboration. It's quick and easy when you do your thinking in advance and plan your supporting points. Doing it this way sets you up to write faster. Instantly, you'll have a launching point and your overall scope defined – so you're more likely to stay on track. Planning provides a guaranteed road map that will get you to the finish line faster.

Select the planning tools or methods that you're most comfortable with. I prefer to map out my content on a pad of paper with a Blue Pilot Hi-Tecpoint V-5 Grip pen. But you should use whatever works for you. Typically I fill about a half to a full page per article, but that's because I prefer the process of mind mapping vs. linear planning or outlining. Again, it's a matter of preference. When the ideas are flowing fast and furiously, you want to seize the moment and scoop them all.

State your article concept clearly and quickly. Next, generate three or more supporting ideas or keywords terms. Now take a look at what you have. Essentially, you now have the structure of your article right in front of you.

If so, there's absolutely no need to complicate it by adding more, unless you're planning a longer article. Now take this basic plan and write the article now, or put it aside while you're in the planning mode, prepare the framework of your next piece.

Keep your outline simple. An article outline could be as few as four words -- one representing the overall topic and three supporting words suggesting the details you will explain within the body copy. You could also create a mind map consisting of words, methods of emphasis, or images. You could even fill out a page of details, if that works best for you. But keep in mind that the more elaborate your outline, the more time you'll have invested – and it's only one article.

Consistently take action. Follow through by doing the necessary work. Any outline, plan, or map is all you need to craft an interesting and informative article. So don't stop until it's written. Give any outline to 100 different writers and you'll get back 100 different articles. That means that each outline could form the basis of multiple, unique articles for you. Just make each separate effort an original, clear and helpful composition – and your efforts will pay dividends.

Channel your thinking. Make your topic specific. The clearer you can define the scope of your piece, the easier it can be to write. That's why creating a basic map or outline is so important; it funnels your thinking and gives you a foundation to build upon. It helps you to clearly see the subject before you. Only when the concept is crystal clear in your mind can you communicate your message with absolute clarity and efficiency.

Arrange the steps in sequence. When planning an article, one method is to use a "chain of thought" process. This is where one idea or step naturally connects to the next. List the items in an orderly sequence. "First you do this... than you do that... and finally, there's this important step to complete the process". Make it easy to follow along.

Plan dozens of articles at once and you'll save time. Start with a list of general topics and then break it down into specifics. Imagine that you're writing a book on your subject area. First you would need ten to thirty major chapter topics. Then each of those chapters could be broken down into ten to thirty separate sub-topics. Each sub-topic is potentially an article. Start with broad strokes and then determine the details. Focus on one important detail and expand upon it with related elements and insights.

Let your outline be your guide.

It's not the intention of the outline to make your writing rigid and boring. Its sole purpose is to give you a roadmap so that when you reach the end, you've crafted an article that makes sense and has value.

Without a plan or map, your writing will wander. But with a basic structure outlined, you can write creatively without feeling handcuffed.

Writing anything is partly about discovering things as you go and you need that freedom to create a compelling piece. But even a basic plan helps to ensure that your free expression is channelled in the right direction and within the parameters of the outline.

Use outlines to boost your writing speed. Outlines give you a jump-start -- without the usual stopping and starting – and this can be a wonderful thing. There's no wondering what to write next because you can see the project and direction clearly. Even the simplest plan is enough to propel you forward at greater speeds. At the same time, your outline gives you the freedom to write whatever comes to mind. It's freedom with a purpose. To write your article quickly, you need to know where you're going. An outline moves you steadily towards completion.

Plant the idea of your article firmly in your mind. Imagine it as a finished piece of approximately 5-10 (or more) well-written paragraphs. List your topic in a single word or sentence and shape it into a title that reads like a headline. Now think about the main idea you want to convey. Write down any keywords or terms, concepts, steps, methods, or relevant questions. Next, discuss those words, concepts, steps and questions listed in conversational form. Talk (or type) your ideas onto the page and let them take shape in sentence form, naturally. Capture your descriptive thoughts as they come and address each important point.

Crystallizing your thoughts before writing can make a world of difference in your article writing productivity. When you break it down into simple steps, you harness ideas quickly and with little effort. It only takes moments to map out a simple article and doing it rapidly, ensures that you don't overcomplicate the idea. Those few moments establish a footing -- a solid foundation for your article. This simple outline shows you the way to share your information. But it's your writing that makes it an enjoyable and valuable trip for the reader.

Communication

Reshape your existing work. Take any article topic you've already covered in outline form and recast it in a different direction. Look beyond the obvious points that came to mind earlier. Take a wider look. Or choose a narrower but deeper view. Twist it around. Look at things in a new way, from a different direction, or an alternate perspective. Invariably, you'll uncover additional topic ideas.

Communicate with clarity. It's not so much what is said that counts, but what is heard. Remember, writing quality, unique articles is about sharing helpful information clearly. Your job as article writer is to convey your information in a way the reader comprehends. The question to ask is: *how can you communicate your key points in a way that she understands the concept as much as you do?*

Inject emotion into your writing. Convey your information more effectively with passion. Having a genuine interest in your subject makes this easy. You've got lessons to share and valuable insights that can make a difference in your reader's life. Now, deliver your information as powerfully as you can to make your point. Put energy and emotion into it and you'll achieve your objective of attracting readers and triggering clicks.

Speak to an audience of one. Make your article interesting and direct. You want it to feel like you're talking one-on-one with your reader. Use mostly short paragraphs for easier reading, but don't hesitate to mix in the odd, slightly longer paragraph too. The occasional paragraph that's one short sentence or even just one word can be very effective. It keeps the reader moving through your material at a good pace and the faster they read, the more they'll appreciate taking the time to do so. Mix it up. If the message is strong, readers will continue reading. Think of your article as a drive through the country with hills and valleys, twists and turns. That's what makes it interesting.

Evoke images in the minds of readers. Tell them and they'll snore. Show them and they'll adore you. As an article writer, the only real tools you have at your disposal are words and how you position them. Your mission is to convey information; to communicate your ideas as mental pictures through the selection and arrangement of your words. To do so precisely, use specific words that conjure clear and vibrant images.

Inject metaphors to help your readers understand the message. A metaphor substitutes one idea, object, or concept with another. As an article writer, you're teaching a lesson and you want every reader to get the message. By likening an idea to something else that's easily visualized, you facilitate the process and simplify the understanding of your content.

Share ideas with confidence, energy, passion and enthusiasm. Think of your content as having a great conversation with someone close to you. You found information of interest or significance and you want to share it. Use any tool from your bag of tricks - stories, analogies, re-living a memorable moment, or sharing a specific experience or result.

Timing

Set a deadline for each article. If you're planning on three to five paragraphs of content and a five minute deadline seems unattainable, allow yourself more time. Start with fifteen or twenty minute articles and then work at incrementally reducing the allowable writing time. You can attain breakthrough speeds when you follow these methods and work with a deadline.

The best way to monitor your time is with a simple kitchen timer. Another option is to use the free online timer – like one at online-stopwatch.com. Whatever version you use, discipline yourself to stick to your predetermined limits and you'll force yourself to become a better and more productive article writer.

Use time as leverage. A deadline increases the pressure, but it also forces you into a sharper level of focus. It's this precise thinking and expression of your ideas that allows you to write quality and unique articles fast. Set your timer and make the commitment to follow through. Force your mind to hold nothing back and to give up the best material first. The more you do this, the easier it gets. Eventually your mind stops fighting and collaborates fully.

Work without interruption. Never stop to edit, until you are finished writing. No matter what you write, there's always another way to say it. When you stop writing to look for a way to fix a passage, it eats up valuable time and cuts in your productivity. Don't spend more time than necessary editing your work and never edit until the writing is complete.

Act swiftly on new ideas. As you take on a new topic - whether it's in single-word form or a fully-descriptive title, you need to give it some shape before writing. When you first consider a topic, it's like holding a hot potato in your hand. You should do something with it immediately. Act fast and find a way that will help your reader grasp the idea. Serve others by providing useful information and you'll turn your article into something of value.

Write your article as fast as you can.

The faster you write, the more naturally you communicate. Get your thoughts down as rapidly as possible and you'll find yourself producing highly-readable writing. Just write it as you would say it. Don't worry about grammar or spelling or any of that. Just communicate your points - one after another - as fast as you can. The faster you can get those words on the page, the better it is for all concerned. Leave the editing for later.

Press on until your article is complete. When you slow down, you interrupt your momentum and flow. When you let your analytical mind get in the way by focusing on the words and how to use them, you become separated from the message. Keep writing rapidly until your article is complete. You can always adjust the wording later, if need be.

Make your point and move on. Speed writing is lean writing. You don't add unnecessary fluff to your words because you're focused on communicating a singular idea in the best possible way. Writing fast forces you to say it succinctly.

Practice over time and your skill and speed will improve. Like most things in life, the more you do it, the easier it gets. The first (or next) article you produce might take you a whopping thirty minutes. That doesn't matter. Just keep going. Apply these ideas and I guarantee you'll write faster than you ever did before. It's just a matter of getting familiar with the techniques and putting them into action daily.

Pace yourself. Find out how you work best and adapt your plan accordingly. Start at a comfortable pace of around fifteen minutes for each one. Plan your work and then work your plan. Write rapidly and as you do, notice the smooth flow you experience. It's exhilarating! Keep it up and you'll eventually find your optimal speed. Strive to reach or better this speed whenever you begin again on another piece of content.

Every minute counts. It's important to monitor the time you invest in article writing. Stick to this proven system and you'll be writing at maximum effectiveness. The secrets are to decide on your path and to keep it simple. Use the idea triggers provided to nail down a topic whenever you need one. Then allow your mind to express itself creatively with your unique flair. Systematically move through each step in the process and by default, your article writing speed will increase exponentially. Additionally, you'll write with greater clarity, conviction and impact. You'll become an article writing dynamo.

Write in short sessions. Thirty to sixty minute periods of high-intensity writing produce quality articles in numbers. This doesn't just work for articles, but for all kinds of content including books, reports and course manuals.

Writing this way forces you to focus and communicate in a direct way that gets the job done. You stick with it until you've made your point and then move on to the next article. It puts you into a productive stream where there's no time for excuses. And limiting the length of your writing sessions helps keep your mind fresh and engaged.

Don't forget to take regular breaks. Reach your article writing goal and then give yourself a rest. No one can write effectively, non-stop, all day long. By all means -- push yourself. But don't overdo it. If you try to force your writing, you'll only grow increasingly frustrated. Taking frequent breaks is refreshing to your body and brain. It's a chance to recover, replenish and re-energize. Use your breaks effectively by doing other, non-writing tasks and you'll find when you get back to writing that you're much more purposeful and effective.

One way to use breaks effectively is to get up and go for a walk. Exercise is an ideal way to give your brain a rest. Detach from the process altogether after an intensive writing session of thirty minutes or longer. If you stay at your computer to check emails, log into accounts, or surf the web, you're not allowing the mental diversion necessary to fully recharge your batteries for your next focused writing gig. Separate yourself completely and you'll come back more relaxed, more focused and more inspired.

Make writing part of your scheduled routine. Contribute significantly to your success every day by writing and submitting just one quality article. As you increase production, the payoff expands exponentially.

Beware of the silent killer called procrastination. Don't just "think" about writing articles. Instead, follow through. You have a proven article speed-writing system in your hands, but it won't do you any good unless you use it. Procrastination is inaction. Any steps taken help to break that inertia. Write articles regularly and the easier it becomes.

Keep moving forward. Forget about perfecting what you've written before getting it out there in the world. Give it your best shot and move on. Perfection doesn't exist, yet it can hold you back and keep you from reaching your full writing potential. Get it written. Make your message as clear as can be and then move onto the next article. Continuous tweaking is wasted time that could be spent far more productively.

Topics and Research

Try to define each article subject succinctly. State it in one line - maximum. Refine it down to its most basic level. What you're looking for is the core idea -- and that's it. It's this specific topic to which your subsequent material will directly relate. You can always revise, refine, or recast any concept into a powerful title. But it's of the utmost importance to just get your big idea onto the page. Ideas are fleeting. If you don't capture them immediately, you either retain only watered-down versions, or lose them altogether.

Entering market niches in which you have a personal interest makes writing content easier on you and more interesting for the reader. If you're writing about a subject that's unappealing to you personally, the task becomes a chore. And if it's difficult to write, imagine what it's like for the poor reader. Enjoy your subject and the words flow with greater ease.

Select topics that are important to you. Share ideas that have made a positive difference for you or someone you know. When you're excited about sharing your discoveries, it's easy to get the words out effectively. The stronger your feelings about the breakthrough information you've discovered, the easier it is to write an article that's well-received.

Expand your thinking. When you explore a subject on a deeper level, new ideas emerge. After you've uncovered your primary points, digging deeper can unearth additional gems. When you let one idea trigger another, the results can be amazing. It's up to you as to whether you include these in the existing article or capture new ideas as they come and craft an additional article based on this new insight or perspective.

Conduct relevant research to build your knowledge base. If you're short on information on your topic or niche, it's time to do some research. Best to have an overall understanding of the general topic before mapping out specific lessons you're going to share in the form of articles. Gather multiple information resources. Pour over them. Discover more about your subject and then let this deeper level of understanding emerge in your writing.

Look for content inspiration everywhere. News channels advertise upcoming shows with attention-grabbing headlines. You can find great topic ideas by scanning the headlines on major web sites like Yahoo, Bing, or RefDesk.com. Magazines rely on this same approach to lure buyers from their visual covers on newsstands. Take a look at any popular consumer magazine available and you'll see clever, sharp, eye-grabbing headlines as article titles. When you're stuck for ideas, a quick trip to the magazine section of a large bookstore can help in a big way.

Become somewhat of an expert in your market niche before taking on the task of writing articles and life is a whole lot easier.

You can get up to speed quickly by devouring top books and information products on the subject. Whatever market you pursue, gain a foundational understanding first. Here's where speed-readers have a distinct advantage. Ask top experts about their best picks for books or courses. Then choose several of the best resources you can find and devour them. If this information is available as audio CD's or MP3's, you can listen while you drive. Within a few weeks, you'll know more about the main topic than most people.

I advise anyone who will listen to make learning a lifelong pursuit. That's what all top performers do and with this kind of knowledge base, writing multiple articles is a breeze.

Read more. Regular reading on your subject and other areas helps you develop fresh article content on an ongoing basis. As you read, mark important points in the text with a pencil. Later you can transfer simple point-form notes to a notebook, which you can in turn use as article fodder.

Consider the information from your target reader's perspective. What's interesting about this to my reader?

What questions would readers likely have about it? Write it down and use it to stimulate future topic ideas.

Editing

Review your article and look for obvious spelling errors first. You'll want to correct any glaring mistakes before posting your article. (This is easy advice to give, but no matter how often I try to catch everything, spelling mistakes still fall between the cracks. If you spot one anywhere in this book, please let me know about it by email and if you're the first, I'll send you a free gift.)

Next, look for the logical presentation of your main idea.

When reading we naturally look for connections that make sense. Your readers will consume your article with their logic filter turned on, so it needs to make sense. Follow a logical, progressive flow from point A to point B and so on. What you've written should carry the reader though the article and straight to your resource box or link. Any stray ideas that obstruct this path should be removed during the editing stage.

Simplify your message to make your ideas easier to understand. Focus on establishing simple and clear communication during the editing phase. Eliminate words and sentences that contribute nothing or get in the way of the direct delivery of your information. But don't spend too much time here or you'll defeat the purpose of speed writing. Shape your words to best express your idea and then move on to the next article in line.

Edit articles in batches. Bundle a number of articles together before beginning the task of editing. Edit one article after another. If you only do one and then go back to brainstorming or writing, overall productivity will suffer. Strengthen your writing in highly-focused review periods of ten to fifteen minutes. Work in blocks of time and do this one task on multiple projects or articles.

Review how your article is constructed. If your article isn't as strong as it could be, take a look at your sentence construction. **Remember: every single sentence either holds or releases your reader's attention.** Ensure that each line contributes meaning and value. Try breaking up a long sentence into two, or combine ideas into one stronger sentence.

Design your article for easy readability. There's not much you can do about the overall design of the page where your article will appear (assuming you're posting it to an article directory or blog). But you can usually control the presentation of the text. Allow a single space between paragraphs. It's the same thing with numbered lists or bullet points. A little "white space" goes a long way towards making the article easier on the reader's eyes. But beware of extra space between your content and resource box. Ideally, they should be one and the same.

Article Writing Templates

Article Idea Starters

Article Title Templates
Article Introduction Templates
 Article Content Idea Triggers
Article Conclusion Templates
Keywords Into Titles
Resource Box Swipe File
Action Words

Article Idea Starters

7-Day

7-Step

101 Ways To

Absolute

Ancient Secrets

Automatic

Beginner's Guide

Blueprint

Breakthrough

Closely-Held Secrets

Course

Crucial

Defined

Easy

Expert

Explained

Explosive

Exposed

For Fun and Profit

Formula

Gaffs

Get Started

Guide

Handbook

Hidden

Home Study

How To

How You Can

Important

In Just 7 Days

Industry Insider

Inside Secrets

Insider

Insights

Insights

Instant

Instantly

Introducing

✓ Irresistible

Key Points

Keys

Made Easy

Magic

Mastery

Mistakes

Mouth-watering

✓ Must Have

Off-Limits

Outline

Overnight

Plan

Private

Profits

Program

Questions

Quick-Fix

Quick Start Guide

Quick and Easy

Red Flag

Restricted

Revealed

Rip-offs

✓ Secrets

Simple

Starting Point

✓ Step By Step

Strategies

Summary

System

Tactics

Techniques

The Art Of

The Dirty Little Secret

The Lazy Way

The One Thing

The Truth About

Tipping Point

Tips

Toolbox

Toolkit

Tools

Turning Point

Ultimate

Ultimate Guide To

Uncovered

Uncut

Unknown

Unveiled

Mistakes

Vital

Warning Signs

Warning

Article Title/Subtitle Templates

(Desired Result) In Just 7 Steps...

(Desired Result) In Only 30 Minutes A Day...

(Desired Result) Without Any Previous Experience...

(Desired Result) Without Endlessly Spending Crazy Amounts Of Money...

(Desired Result) Without Inside Contacts...

(Desired Result) Without Pain...

(Desired Result) Without Special Skills...

(Method or Technique) Of The (Top Achievers in Market) And...

(Option #1) Vs. (Option #2): How To Make The Best Choice For You...

(Option #1) Vs. (Option #2): What's The Difference?...

(Option #1) Vs. (Option #2): Which Makes More Sense For You?...

(Quantity of Principles, Steps, Critical Ideas, etc) You Must Know To...

(Quantity of Qualifications) You Need To...

(Quantity of Something) You Should Avoid If...

(Quantity of Something) You Should Grab If...

(Subject's) Greatest Secret...

√ (Subject): One Of The Most Vital Steps To...

(Subject): What It Is And How It Works...

(Subject) Breakthroughs...

(Subject) Breakthroughs That Can Give You...

(Subject) Breakthroughs That Can Transform Your...

(Subject) Breakthroughs To Slash Your...

(Subject) Checklist...

(Subject) For (Specific Target Market)

(Subject) For Beginners...

(Subject) For Busy (Specific Target Market)

(Subject) For Fun And Profit...

(Subject) For Stressed-Out (Specific Target Market)

(Subject) Ideas 101...

(Subject) In A Nutshell...

(Subject) Is Easier Than You Think

(Subject) Is So Simple Even A...

(Subject) Is The Next Best Thing To...

(Subject) Made Easy: 3 Quick Tips To...

(Subject) Makes (Desired Results) Convenient...

(Subject) Makes (Desired Results) Easier...

(Subject) Makes (Desired Results) Faster...

(Subject) Makes (Desired Results) More Trouble-Free...

(Subject) Makes (Undesired Results) Disappear...

(Subject) Makes Life Easier By...

(Subject) Re-examined: Is It All It's Cracked Up To Be?...

(Subject) Starts Working Instantly...

(Subject) The Easy Way...

(Subject) The Easy Way In Just...

(Subject) The Quick and Easy Way...

(Subject) Without The Usual Problems...

(Topic): What It Really Takes To...

2 Essential Skills You Must Possess If...

3 "Copy and Paste" (Subject) Templates...

3 "No-Brainer" Ways To...

3 "Plug and Play" Sessions To...

3 (Desired Results) Almost No One Knows About...

3 (Items) To Avoid If You Want to...

3 (Subject) Advantages You Already Have But Might Not Be Using...

✓ 3 (Subject) Lessons From (An Unlikely or Unusual Source)...

✓ 3 (Subject) Methods That Work Every Time...

✓ 3 (Subject) Secrets I Learned From (Expert or Unexpected Source)...

3 (Subject) Secrets You Can Legally Steal To...

3 Advanced (Subject) Techniques That Can...

✓ 3 Advantages That Will Give You...

3 Basic Tools You Must Have To Succeed At...

✓ 3 Big Benefits Of...

3 Blunders Nearly Everyone Makes When...

3 Critical Tricks...

3 Different Types Of (Subject) And How...

3 Dirt Cheap Methods That Could...

3 Easy Jumpstart Methods To...

3 Emotional Triggers That Get People To...

149

3 Essential Elements Of An Effective...

3 Fast-Track Ways To...

3 Fill-In-The-Blanks Solutions For To Use Whenever...

3 Fresh Approaches To...

3 Good Reasons...

3 Good Reasons Why...

3 Guaranteed Ways To...

3 Guerrilla Tactics To...

3 Hidden Benefits Of...

3 High-Powered (Subject) Tips You've Never Heard Before...

3 Idea Prompts For (Specific Market) Who Sometimes Get Stuck...

3 Ideas For Making More Money With...

3 Ideas You Can Legally Steal To...

3 In-The-Trenches Secrets For...

3 Inside Advantages You Need To...

3 Inside Secrets To (Subject) That Nobody Wants To Tell You...

3 Insights That Can...

3 Keys Everyone Wants To Know About...

3 Little-Known (Subject) Tactics That Work Big-Time...

3 Little-Known Ways To...

3 Money-Saving Ways To...

3 Must-Have...

3 Often Overlooked Things To Consider When...

3 Pitfalls To Success In...

3 Questions Almost Everyone Asks About...

3 Questions To Ask Before...

3 Reasons Why...

3 Reasons Why Experts Advise...

3 Reasons Why You Should...

3 Rules Of...

3 Secrets To...

3 Shortcuts To Mastering...

3 Signs It's Time To...

3 Simple Guidelines To Better...

3 Simple Shortcuts For Mastering...

3 Simple Shortcuts To Get Great Results With...

3 Simple Strategies For...

3 Simple Strategies For Success In...

3 Simple Tricks For...

3 Simple Variations That...

3 Skills You Need To..

3 Starter Questions to Ask Yourself Before...

3 Starter Steps To Get You Up And Running In...

3 Steps To...

3 Strategies For Overcoming...

3 Stupid Things Some (Target Prospects) Do When...

3 Telltale Signs...

3 Things To Look For In...

3 Things You Must Never...

3 Time-Saving Tricks To...

3 Time-Saving Ways To...

3 Time-Tested Techniques Guaranteed To...

3 Tips For Better...

3 Tips To Handle Any...

3 Tips To Help You (Achieve Results) Almost Instantly...

3 Top-Secret Resources For...

3 Top Secret Techniques For...

3 Valuable Lessons Learned From...

3 Ways To...

3 Ways To Automatically (Achieve Desired Benefit)...

3 Ways To Cheat...

3 Ways To Replace (Subject) And...

3 Ways You Can (Get Results) When You Need To...

3 Ways to Get Results Faster From...

3 Winning Concepts For...

5 "Last Lecture" Lessons To Help You...

5 (Subject) Ideas That Will Multiply Your...

5 (specific benefit) Tips Almost Nobody Knows About...

5 Actions You Could Take Immediately When...

5 Barriers That Get In Way Of...

5 Certain Signs You Are...

5 Closely-Guarded Secrets Of...

5 Critical Components Of...

5 Easy Ways To Prevent...

5 Get-Started Tips For Struggling...

5 Hidden Barriers To...

5 Indicators Your (Subject) Needs...

5 Low Cost/No Cost Ways To...

5 Must-Have Resources For...

5 Secrets To...

5 Simple, Fill-In-The-Blank...

5 Simple Solutions To...

5 Simple Steps For...

5 Simple Steps To Crafting...

5 Simple Strategies For...

5 Specific Tips To...

5 Street-Smart Tactics To Help You...

5 Stupid Things People Do When...

5 Sure-fire Ways To...

5 Time-Saving Tips For...

5 Tips For...

5 Tips To...

5 Under-Used (Subject) Strategies Just Waiting...

5 Ways To (Benefit #1) and (Benefit #2)...

5 Ways To...

5 Ways To Resolve...

5 Ways You Can...

5 Winning Ideas Found At...

7 (Time/Money/Energy) Saving Ways To...

7 Days To...

7 Fastest Solutions For...

7 Habits Of Highly-Successful...

7 Instant Ideas For...

7 Key Factors To...

7 Most Cost-Effective Ways To...

7 One-Minute Steps To Ensure...

7 Powerful Advantages Of...

7 Proven Steps...

7 Short Days To...

7 Sure-Fire Ways To...

7 Top Tips For...

7 Ways To (Attain Benefit) In Any...

7 Ways To (Attain Results) With...

7 Ways To (Attain Results) Without...

7 Ways To Find Anything By...

7 Winning Ways To Get Started...

7-Point Checklist For...

21 Days To (Subject) Breakthrough Results Even If You're A Complete Beginner...

21 Days To (Subject) Success...

60-Second Secrets Of...

A (Target Market)'s Guide To (Desired Result)...

A 5-Day Plan For...

A 7-Day Plan For...

A Cheat Sheet Shortcut To...

A Checklist For...

A Crash Course In...

A Dirt-Cheap, Simple, Do-It-Yourself Way To...

A Field Guide To...

A Lesson In (Subject) From (An Unlikely Source)...

A Newcomers Guide To...

A Quick Guide To...

A Quick Overview Of The Most Important...

A Quick Refresher For...

A Rarely-Used But Highly-Effective Technique For...

A Safe, Easy Way To...

A Secret Method For...

A Simple Solution To...

A Simple Technique That Virtually Guarantees...

A Surprisingly Simply Way To...

A Tale From...

A Tiny Little (Subject) Technique That...

A Wickedly-Simple Way To...

A Word Of Caution About...

Add This To Your...

Advanced (Subject) Secrets For...

Advanced (Subject) Strategies: How To Blast Past...

Advanced (Target Market) Guide To...

Advanced Methods Of (Subject) To (Achieve Great Results) In Half The Time...

Advantages and Disadvantages of...

Advice (Experts or Authority Figures) Give To...

Advice To (Target Market) From...

Advice To...

After All The...

Age-Old (Subject) Secrets You Can Still Use Today...

The A-B-C Guide To...

An Amazing, All-Purpose...

An Astonishingly Productive Way To...

An Exact Blueprint Of...

An Important Caveat About...

An Important Point About...

An Ingenious Way To...

An Innovative Solution For...

An Original Technique For...

Another Method Of...

Another Way To...

Are You...

Are You Confident Enough To...?

Are You Cut Out To Be...?

Are You Ready For (Specific Action)? Test Yourself...

Are You Ready For...

Are You Ready To (Specific Action)? Here's How To Know...

Are You Thinking About...?

Ask A Top (Expert) About (Subject) And You'll Discover...

Ask An Expert About...

Astounding New (Subject) Secrets...

At Last A (Subject) Solution That Works...

Automatic Techniques To...

Avoiding The 3 Most Common (Subject) Mistakes...

Basic (Subject) Primer For Beginners...

Basics Of (Subject) Revealed...

Becoming A Successful (Subject) Means...

Best Kept Secrets Of...

Best Of All Tips For...

Break The (Subject) Cycle...

Break The (Subject) Cycle Fast and Forever...

Break The (Subject) Cycle Once And For All...

Break The (Subject) Cycle With These Proven Tips...

Break The (Subject) Habit – Here's How...

Breakthrough (Subject): 3 Must-Have Essentials To Jumpstart Your Success

Can You Really (Attain Desired Outcome) In Just...

Changing The Way You Think About (Subject)...

Check Out What (Authority Figures) Don't Tell You About...

Closely-Guarded Secrets Of...

Clues Reveal...

Common Mistakes To Avoid When...

Confessions Of A...

Confessions Of A One-Time...

Confessions Of A Reformed...

Consider What Happens When...

Conventional Wisdom About (Subject) May Be Wrong: Here's Why...

Cool (Subject) Ideas For...

Copy These Sure-fire Techniques And...

Could This Be...?

Cures For...

Dealing With...

Discover How To...

Discover The Easiest Way Ever To...

Discover The Fast-Track To...

Discover The Magic Of...

Discovering (Subject) Benefits You 3 Ways...

Discovering (Subject) Can Actually Be Easy...

Do This And Instantly Improve...

Do You...

Do You Have...?

Do You Have The Courage To (Specific Action) Even Though...?

Do You Have The Guts To...?

Do You Have To Courage To...?

Do You Have What It Takes To...?

Do You Qualify For...?

Does (Typical Action Taken) Give You Chills?

Don't Even Think About (Specific Action) If You Want...

Don't Forget About...

Don't Read This If...

Do NOT Read This If You've Already Mastered The Secrets Of...

Don't Worry About...

Dumb (Subject) Mistakes That Can...

Early Warning Signs Of...

Easily Defeat Any (Problem Related To Market)...

Effective (Subject): 3 Reasons To...

Effective (Subject): 3 Things You Must Do...

Enjoy The Ultimate...

Everything I Know About (Subject)... I Learned From (Unexpected Source)...

Everything I Know About (Subject) I Learned From...

Everything You Need To...

Everything You Need To Know About...

Experience Not Required: Here's How To...

Experience The Thrill Of...

Expert Reveals...

Facts You...

Facts You Might Have...

Favourite Stealth Secrets Of...

Finally, The Truth About...

Finding The Fastest Methods Of...

Finding Your (Subject) Groove Can...

First Steps To...

Foolproof Techniques For...

For Busy People Who...

Free Examples Of...

Frequently Asked Questions About (Subject) And The Shocking Answers...

Fun And Exciting Activities For...

Fun And Exciting Ways To...

Get More (Desired Results) The Easy Way...

Getting Started In...

Getting Started With...

Hassle-Free Ways To...

Have You Ever...

Here's How Easy It Is To...

Here's More...

Here's Proof That...

Here's Something Else That's Going To...

Here's Why You Must...

Here's Your Chance To...

Hire A Pro And...

Home Remedies For...

How (Someone Within Target Market) Created (Results) And How You Can Too...

How (Subject) Helps (Target Market) Get Superior Results...

How (Subject) Helps You At Least 3 Ways...

How (Subject) Helps You To...

How...

How A Simple In (Subject) Shift Can...

How An Ordinary Item That Costs Less Than...

How Current Trends Could Affect Your...

How I (Achieved Big Results) And How You Can Too...

How I (Achieved Result) In Just 90 Days As A...

How I (Achieved Specific Results)...

How I...

How Is It Possible To...?

How Much...

How One (Target Market) Used (Basic Thing Of Idea) To...

How Safe Is...

How The Pros (Specific Action) and What You Can Learn By Watching Them...

How To (Accomplish Great Things) Even If...

How To (Achieve Benefit) Before...

How To (Achieve Specific Result) Before...

How To (Achieve Specific Result) By Lunchtime Tomorrow...

How To (Acquire or Attain) Your First...

How To (Attain Desired Result) Cheaply Or Even For Free...

How To (Attain Desired Result) Quickly and Easily...

How To (Attain Desired Result) Without Any Experience...

How To (Attain Desired Result) Without Paying A Penny...

How To (Attain Desired Result) Without Spending A Fortune...

How To (Attain Result) In Half The Time...

How To (Attain Results) In Only 24 Hours...

How To (Attain Results) With Virtually No...

How To (Attain a Specific Benefit) In Just 7 Days

How To (Benefit #1) And (Benefit #2)...

How To (Make, Design, Build) A (Subject) In 5 Easy Steps...

How To (Obtain Desired Result) In Just 21 Days...

How To (Obtain Desired Result) With (Subject)...

How To (Specific Action) And Still Get The Results You Want...

How To (Specific Action) Like A (Recognized Expert)...

How To...

How To Achieve...

How To Attract...

How To Beat...

How To Blast Past The 3 Most Common Challenges Facing New (Target Market) Today...

How To Boost...

How To Bypass The Usual Learning Curve And...

How To Create...

How To Deal With...

How To Decrease...

How To Earn...

How To Effortlessly...

How To Find...

How To Finish...

How To Free Yourself From...

How To Get (Benefit) Without...

How To Get Better (Subject) Results Than Anyone, Anywhere, Anytime...

How To Get More...

How To Get Out Of...

How To Get Over...

How To Get Through The...

How To Increase...

How To Launch...

How To Lose...

How To Make (Result) With Just...

How To Make...

How To Make Money With...

How To Never Again...

How To Organize A...

How To Overcome...

How To Overcome The 3 Barriers That All...

How To Overturn...

How To Profit...

How To Profit From...

How To Quickly And Easily Get More...

How To Quickly and Easily Stop...

How To Reverse...

How To Save...

How To Seize...

How To Skip A Few Steps And...

How To Skip The Grunt Work And...

How To Start...

How To Start With Nothing And...

How To Survive...

How To Survive Your First Day...

How To Take Advantage Of...

How To Teach...

How To Train...

How To Turn...

How To Uncover...

How To Use...

How To Win...

How To Win In...

How Would (Expert, Recognized Authority, or Historical Figure) Have...

How You Can...

If You're Worried About...

If You Have...

If You Want (Desired Result) Here's Good News...

Imagine...

Imagine You - A Successful...

Important Lessons From...

Impossible To (Attain Desired Result)? No and Here's Why...

In Short, Here's All You Need To...

Inexpensive Resources To Help You...

Inside Secrets Of...

Instant (Subject) Results...

Instant Tactics That Practically Force...

Is It Bad To...

Is It Embarrassing When...?

Is It Really Wise To...?

Is It Self-Defeating To...

Is It Wrong To Want...

Just Wait Until...

Kick-Start Your...

Know This And...

Learn How (Experts) Train To...

Learn How One (Target Market) Achieved Great Results...

Learn To (Subject) Like A Pro...

Learn To...

Less (Subject) Means More (Positive Results) For...

Let's Suppose...

Let Me Give You My...

Let Me Share A Valuable Secret About (Subject) With You...

Let Me Show You How (Subject) Works...

Live Like...

Make The Most Of...

Mastering (Subject) In Just...

Maximum (Desired Benefit) Tricks That Will...

Maximum (Desired Results) Secrets...

Mistakes To Avoid With...

Money-Saving Ways To...

More Tips For...

My Top 3 Tips For...

My Top Tips For...

New (Subject) System Makes (Getting Results) Easier Than...

New, Highly-Effective Method To...

New Breakthrough Formula...

New Breakthrough In (Subject) Means...

No-Nonsense Advice About...

Not Knowing The Rules Of (Subject) Could Cost You...

One Idea That...

One More Thing...

One More Thing About...

One More Thing You Need...

One Shift Can...

Perfect (Desired Result) Every Time, The Easy Way...

Perfect (Desired Result) For Less Than...

Perfect (Desired Result) In Minutes...

Perfect (Desired Result) Made Easy...

Poor (Specific) Skills - A Major Obstacle To (Subject) Success...

Preventable (Subject) Mistakes That Can Cost You A Fortune...

Professional Results With...

Profit From The Ultimate...

Protect Your (Something Audience Values) From...

Proven Success Model For...

Quick-Fixes For...

Quick And Easy Ways To Improve Your...

Quick And Helpful Ideas For...

Quick-Start Success Secrets...

Rapid (Desired Solution) Results In...

Rapid Results: How To (Get Result) Faster Than...

Ready, Set, Go: 3 Steps To Get Your (Subject) Started Right...

Remedies For...

Say Goodbye To...

Secret Confessions Of A Master (Target Market) Make It...

Secrets Of The...

Secrets Of The Highest-Paid (Target Market)...

Secrets Of The Pros...

Secrets Of World-Class (Target Market)...

Secrets Of World-Class...

Secrets To Successful...

Select Ways To...

Shortcuts For (Target Prospect) - How To...

Should You...

Simple But Powerful...

Skeptical About _____? You Should Be...

Something You Probably Don't Know About...

Sorry, But I've Got To Tell The Truth About...

Sorry To Burst Your Bubble About...

Special Techniques That Instantly Gives You...

Specific Tips About...

Spilling The Beans About...

Starting A (Subject) The Right Way...

Starting Off With...

Steal This And...

Success Secrets For...

Success Tips For...

Successful (Subject) In The World Today...

Super-Advanced Formula For...

Super-Effective Ways To...

Super-Fast Ways To...

Super-Quick Methods Of...

Sure-fire Techniques To...

Surprising New Discovery...

Take Advantage Of...

Take One Moment To...

Taking (Subject) A Step Further...

Taking (Subject) To The Limit...

Taking A Closer Look At...

The #1 Reason Why...

The (Expert's) Guide To...

The (Method or Technique) Top (Target Market) Use To...

The (Name) Technique: Secret Technique Of The Most...

The (Popular Figure or News Story) Phenomenon And What It Means For...

The (Popular Movie) Method Of...

The (Popular News Item) And What (Target Market) Can Learn From...

The (Popular TV Show) Secrets Of...

The (Pro's or Expert's) 5-Step Guide To Becoming...

The (Professional's or Expert's) Guide To Getting Great (Subject) Results At Home

The (Recognized Group Of Experts like Doctors) 5-Day Formula For...

The (Subject) Hot Sheet For Quick Learning...

The (Subject) Primer...

The (Subject) Secret Others Paid Money For Is Yours Free...

The (Target Prospect's) Guide To Becoming...

The (target audience) Guide To...

The 3 Best Ways To...

The 3 Hidden (Subject) Traps Nobody Tells You About...

The 3 Key Questions To Ask Before...

The 3 Main Disadvantages Of...

The 3 Major Advantages (Taking Specific Action) Gives You...

The 3 Most Common Mistakes (Target Market) Make When (Attempting a Task) And (How To Fix It)...

The 3 Most Difficult Obstacles (Target Market) Face And How To Overcome Them...

The 3 Most Effective (Subject) Methods Ever...

The 3 Surprises You'll Discover When...

The 3 Surprises That Confront Every...

The 3 Things You Should Do When...

The 3-Hour Formula For...

The 3-Minute Short Course On...

The 3-Minute Solution For...

The 3-Step Formula For...

The 5 Basics Of...

The 5 Best Ideas For...

The 5 Easiest Ways To...

The 5 Minute Guide To...

The 7 Best (Subject) For...

The 7 Best Tips For...

The 7-Day Checklist For...

The 7-Day Guide To...

The 10-Point Checklist For...

The Amazing Secrets Of...

The Art Of...

The Basic Elements Of Every...

The Basic Rules Of...

The Basics Of (Subject) You Need To Know To...

The Best (List of Specific Things) Of All Time...

The Best (List of Specific Things) This Year...

The Best (Opportunities) For...

The Best Answers To The Top 3 Questions On...

The Cold, Hard Facts About...

The Common Mistakes Most New (Target Audience)
Make...

The Complete (Subject) Process In 5 Easy Steps...

The Crucial Differences Between...

The Cure-All For...

The Cure For...

The Dirty Little Secret...

The Dumb Mistakes Most (Target Audience) Make When...

The Easiest Way To...

The Easy Way To Plan...

The Essence Of...

The Fast-Action Guide To (Attaining Desire) In Just 14 Days...

The First 3 Steps You Must Take To...

The First Step To...

The First Year Of...

The Frustrated (Target Prospect's) Guide To...

The Hidden Value Of...

The Ideal Way To...

The Importance Of (Subject) In...

The Importance Of...

The Intelligent Way To...

The Joy Of (Specific Result) And How To Experience It More...

The Joy Of (Specific Result) Exposed...

The Joy Of (Specific Result) Made Easy...

The Joy Of...

The Key To...

The Keys To...

The Last Minute Shoppers Guide To...

The Last Minute Solution To...

The Long-Lasting Way To Break The (Subject) Cycle...

The Many Advantages Of...

The Most Important 3 Steps To...

The Number One Reason...

The One Action Step That Can...

The One Basic Ingredient To...

The One Main Reason Why...

The One Secret (Approach To Subject) That Gives You...

The One Thing About (Subject) You Should Never Forget...

The One Thing You Must...

The One Thing You Must Do To...

The One Underlying Secret Most People Miss When It Comes To...

The Only 3 Things (Target Market) Need To Know About...

The Only 3 Things You'll Every Need To...

The Only Real Question To Ask Yourself Before...

The Only Thing You Need To Get (Desired Result) Is...

The Only Things You Need To Remember About...

The Other Things You Need...

The Perfect...

The Perfect Way To (Specific Action)...

The Perfect Way To...

The Plain Truth About...

The Power Of...

The Proven Power Of...

The Quick-Start Resource Guide For...

The Quickest Way To...

The Rapid-Fire Guide To (Attaining Result)...

The Real Kicker When It Comes To...

The Real Truth About...

The Reality About...

The Scary Part About...

The Secret (Subject) Skill You Need And How To Acquire It Fast...

The Secret Of Secrets About...

The Secret That Gives You...

The Secrets Of Using...

The Shocking Truth About...

The Simple Habits Of...

The Single Most Important...

The Single Most Important Step To...

The Smart (Target Audience) Guide To...

The Smart (Target Prospect's) Simple, Step-By-Step Plan For...

The Story Of...

The Thinking Persons Guide To...

The Top 3 (Subject) Tips You've Probably Never Heard Before...

The Top 3 Secrets Of...

The Top 3 Secrets To...

The Top 5 Advantages Of...

The Top 5 Reasons Why You Should...

The Top 5 Recommended Books For...

The Top 5 Recommended Resources For...

The Top 7 Reasons Why Most (Target Market) Fail...

The Truth About...

The Ultimate...

The Ultimate Get Started Tips Guide To...

The Ultimate In...

The Ultimate Shot-Gun Start For...

The World's Best...

The World's Easiest Way To...

There's More To...

There's Nothing Quite Like...

Thousands Have Been...

Time-Saving Ways To...

Time-Tested Techniques For...

Tips For (Attaining Desired Results) In Record Time...

Title Templates

Top 3 (Subject) Secrets For...

Top 3 Favourite (Subject) Techniques Most Pros Use...

Top 3 Methods For...

Top 3 Questions About...

Top 3 Reasons To...

Top 3 Recommended Resources For...

Top 3 Shortcuts To...

Top 3 Ways To...

Top 5 Concerns About...

Top 5 Secrets Of...

Top Secret (Ideas, Solutions, Tactics, etc) For...

Transform Your...

Treat Yourself...

Tricks, Tips And Shortcuts To...

Unlock The Hidden (Subject) Secrets...

Using (Other Options) As A Low Cost Alternative Could...

Warning Signs About (Subject) You May Have
Overlooked...

Warning Signs Of...

Warning Signs That Could...

What's Most Important About...

What's The Answer To...?

What's The Best Way To...?

What's The Catch When It Comes To...?

What (Insiders or Elite Group) Won't Tell You About (Specific Subject)...

What Better Way To...

What Does A Great (Subject) Really Need?

What Every (Member of Target Audience) Needs To Know About...

What Every (Member of Target Audience) Should Know About (Specific Subject)...

What Every (Target Market) Should Know About...

What Every (Target Market) Should Know Before...

What I Learned From (Person, Event, or Experience) About (Subject)...

What I Learned From (Well Known Source) About...

What Is (Subject) Anyway?

What Is A (Subject) And How Can It Help You?

What It Takes To...

What It Takes To Get Started With (Subject) Today And...

What Never To...

What Never To Do If...

What Never To Do In...

What Never To Do When...

What Really Happens When...?

What The Top (Experts) Use To...

What They Won't Tell You About...

What To Do If...

What To Do Now That...

What To Do When...

What To Do When Someone...

What To Do When You're At...

What To Do When You're Frustrated By...

What To Do When You...

What To Do When You Can't Get...

What To Do When You Can't Quite...

What To Do When You Feel...

What To Do When You Need...

What To Do When You Need To...

What To Do When You Simply Must (Achieve a Result) But You...

What To Do When Your...

What To Look For Before...

What To Look For In...

What Would (Historical Figure) Have Done About...

What Would Happen If...

What Would You Do...?

What You Can Do When...

What You Need To Know About...

What You Should Do When...

What You Should Know About...

What Your Gut Feeling...

Whatever You Do...

When Conventional (Field of Experts) Should Be Ignored...

When It Comes To...

Where All The (Top Achievers in Market) Go For...

Where Most (Target Prospects) Get It Wrong...

Where To Find...

Who Else Wants...?

Whoever Thought It Was Difficult...

Why (Alternative) Doesn't As Well As...

Why (Conventional Methods) Don't Work Anymore For...

Why (Target Market) Need To...

Why...

Why 99% Of...

Why Bother (Taking Typical Steps) When You Could...

Why It's Actually Easier To...

Why It's Actually Faster To...

Why It's Almost Always...

Why It's Better To...

Why It's So Important To...

Why Most...

Why The "Standard" Advice About (Subject) Can Actually Harm You...

Why Top (Target Market) Use...

Why You'll Never Find...

Why You Must...

Why You Should...

Why You Should Never...

Why You Shouldn't Even Think About...

Worry-Free (Results) So You Can...

Worry-Free...

Yes You Can...

You'd Never Guess...

You'll Wonder Why...

You've Never Seen...

Your 7-Point (Subject) Checklist...

Your First Move To...

Your Next Move To...

Your Quick-Reference (Subject) Checklist...

Your Quick-Start Guide to...

Your Strongest Hunch About...

Article Introduction Templates

(Subject) is important. But...

Are you concerned about...?

Are you disappointed with...?

Are you dissatisfied with...?

Are you fed up with...?

Are you frustrated with...?

Are you interested in making a difference...?

Are you stressed-out about...?

Are you worried...?

As a (member of specific group) you can...

Ask 10 people what (subject) means to them and...

As you're reading this, other (members of target market) are...

Could this be the one missing piece of the puzzle...?

Could this be the one stumbling block to...?

Could this be the one thing holding you back...?

Did you know...?

Did you know that as (member of a specific group) that you and I are...?

Discover the secrets of (subject) and you can...

Does this result look familiar...?

Does this situation sound familiar...

Do you want to discover...

Do you worry about (subject) whenever...?

Due to...

Exciting? It sure is because...

First you've got to have...

First you need...

Has this ever happened to you or someone you know...?

Has this every happened...

Have you ever...

Have you had enough of...?

Have you heard about...?

Here's the key that will unlock the mystery of...

Here's your chance to...

How would you like to...

How would you like to be able to...?

How would you like to earn...

How would you like to enjoy...

How would you like to have...?

How would you like to make...

How would your life be different if...?

I've found a certain path to (result) and I'd like to share it with you...

I (saved, made, collected, etc) (specific result) by...

If (subject) happened... what would you do...?

If anyone had suggested this...

If at first you don't succeed...

If it hasn't happened yet, it will. But you...

If it hasn't happened to you yet...

If you're like me you have less time than ever for...

If you can (take specific action) than you can (achieve specific results)

If you don't...

If you found (subject) helpful... you'll be interested in...

If you had this information just a few years ago...

If you like (something target market desires)... you'll love...

If you put off (subject)... now is the time because...

I know (subject) will change...

I know this information will...

I know you're busy, but this information can...

Imagine (ultimate benefit of breakthrough results)...

Imagine for a moment...

Imagine having...

Imagine how your life would be different today if...

Imagine this scenario and...

In this article, I'm going to...

In this article, I'm going to let you in on a secret...

In this article, I'm going to show you...

In this article, you're about to...

It's not a question of "if"... but...

It's not as simple as...

It's true. This information (created a specific result) and I know...

It doesn't have to be difficult...

It doesn't take an expert to...

It doesn't take much to...

It happens a lot more than you'd think...

Last month, something happened that will change...

Last month something happened to affect your...

Let me ask you a question. If you...

Look down the road and...

Look just 5 years into the future and...

Many people get it wrong because...

Over 10,000 people can't be wrong...

Prepare yourself for more than a few pleasant surprises...

Stop for a moment and...

The first time I tried this...

The first time I tried this step-by-step method...

The first time I used this information...

The first time I used this strategy, I (saved, earned, made, created, etc.)...

The marketplace is as tough as it's ever been. But that doesn't mean...

There's a very good reason when someone like you...

There's a very good reason why...

There are at least a dozen good reasons I could give you...

There is just one reason to read this article...

This article is different from any other. Why? Because...

This is difficult to write because...

Thousands have tried and failed. But that's because...

Times are tough. But...

What do you do when...?

What happens when...?

What if you had to (achieve a specific result) this month, or else...?

What would you do if...

When you need to...

Where most people go wrong is...

Would answers to any of these questions help you to...?

Yes you can...

You'd think that...

You'd think that after all the years spent...

You're a busy person, so I'll be brief...

You can actually (slash, save, dramatically improve, etc.)...

You have one minute to...

You may be constantly trying to (get a result) but...

You may now enjoy (Specific result) but...

You may now enjoy...

You might think that...

You now have all the information you need to...

You now have a proven formula for...

You really can...

Your interest in (subject) reveals something about you...

Article CONTENT Idea Triggers

3 tips

3 lessons

3 toughest challenges

3 questions that always come up

3 most important things

3 keys

3 secrets

3 ways

3 discoveries

3 methods

3 techniques

3 tactics

3 new ways

3 old ways

3 faster ways

3 cheaper ways

3 foolproof methods

3 dirty little secrets

3 insider secrets

3 timeless ideas

3 simple ideas

3 thirty-second strategies

3 time-saving techniques

3 surprisingly-simple tactics

3 secrets of the pros

3 approaches

3 magic words

3 magic methods

3 most important things

3 steps

3 pieces of the puzzle

3 life lessons

3 takeaways

3 little-known ideas

3 insights

3 twists

3 most common mistakes

3 dangers

3 warning signs

3 pitfalls

Questions To Stimulate Ideas

1. What are the first three ideas that come to mind when you think of this topic? (Simply jot down the words, ideas, thoughts, or images that appear on the screen of your mind.)

2. If you had to describe each of your top three (topic) secrets in just one word, how would you do it? (Think on your feet. Capture the essence of each secret in a single word or phrase.)

3. Name the top three ways most people get it wrong when it comes to this subject. (What are the common blunders people make that keep them from getting the results they really want?)

4. How would others describe the concept or solution to a problem? (A chef might refer to it as a recipe with ingredients and a specific sequence of methods... for a doctor - it might be a prescription with additional actions that need to be taken. When you think in these terms, what potential quick-fixes or longer-term solutions come to mind?)

5. If you had to name the 3 most important components of your topic or sub-topic, what would they be? (Focus on those critical action steps. You're not limited to 3, but 3 is enough for a single article.)

6. How would a child solve this problem? What about a librarian... architect... production manager... mother... or

197

business trainer? What wisdom would an older person with lots of life experience suggest?

7. Identify 3 critical pieces of the puzzle. What are 3 parts, 3 steps, or 3 prerequisites that are required to get the desired results? What about those elements that can enhance the result, but may not be absolutely essential?

8. Divide your topic into 3 by looking at the past, present and future. How was the task completed in the past? How are today's methods different? How will the future change the way things are done today? (Identify the before... the now... and how it might be in years to come and write a paragraph about each.)

9. Reveal how your own methods related to the subject have evolved over time. (First, there was this... and then we did it this way. Now there's a far better approach and this is how we do it today to get the best results.)

10. What 3 words best represent the subject of your article? (Quickly capture three 'word labels' you can assign that describe or summarize your proposed content.)

11. Provide 3 examples that illustrate your concept or thesis. (Make your statement and then provide evidence by sharing examples or case histories.)

12. What are the first 3 steps to take to get you on the right track to accomplish a task or obtain a result? (What actions will move readers closer to the outcome they seek?)

13. What are the last 3 steps that must be completed to maximize results?

14. What are the most overlooked 3 steps, details, or methods that limit people from getting optimum results?

15. What results do you want to help your reader to obtain by reading your article? Is there more than one way to recognize it when you get there?

16. Is there a critical path that must be followed? If so, can it be summarized in just 3 points?

17. What are the next 3 steps in the process? Once completed, what's next after that?

18. What 3 words best describe one element of your sub-topic? (Think of it as 3 magic words - words that summarize the concept, or highlight the most important information for readers.)

Article Conclusion Templates

3 simple steps. That's it. But it means...

Anyone can do this - they really can...

As you've just discovered...

As you can imagine...

As you can see...

As you do this, keep in mind...

As you might imagine...

Avoid, overlook, or ignore these important steps and what you're really doing is...

Can this strategy work just as well for you? You won't know for sure until...

Contrary to popular belief, it doesn't take...

Even if you're sceptical I urge you to...

First you need to understand a new idea. Then you...

Follow these ideas and...

Get ready for more than a few pleasant surprises...

I encourage you to...

If you're fed up with...

If you're serious about...

If you could follow the simple, step-by-step...

If you incorporate...

If you put off (taking a specific action)... now is the time to...

If you take action...

If you take these steps and...

If you take what I've said to heart...

If you try...

If you use...

If you want to...

If you want to leapfrog your way to top of the heap...

If you would only put these steps to the test...

I know this can work for you because...

Imagine enjoying...

Imagine getting the same kind of...

In only 3 steps, you've just discovered...

It's true. These are the exact same steps...

It's true. These very methods are...

It doesn't have to be complicated. In fact, when you keep it simple and...

It sounds good in theory. But when you put this concept to work...

Just remember these 3 secrets whenever...

Just think where you would be today if you had this kind of information...

Lock these 3 nuggets into your memory bank and...

Look, if you can...

Maybe this makes sense to you. Maybe not. But...

Most people don't (achieve a specific result) because...

Prepare yourself for an exciting payoff because...

Prepare yourself for the results that can come to you by...

Quicker. Easier. Cheaper. Those three benefits are yours every time you...

Shocking? Perhaps. But...

Successful (subject) doesn't have to be difficult. Just...

Successful (subject) doesn't have to be expensive. In fact...

Successful (subject) doesn't have to take months of effort. All you need is...

Surprised how easy it can be? Go ahead and...

Take it one step at a time and...

Take these 3 inside secrets and make them your own. What you'll soon discover is...

Take these 5 tips and start using them to...

Take this information and use it. If you do nothing else but add these 3 steps....

That's all there is to it. Just follow...

The (conditions, marketplace, economy, etc.) is as tough as it's ever been. But...

The bottom line is...

The first time I tried this, I...

The information I just shared with you is...

There's no question...

There are hundreds of real success stories...

There you have it...

Thousands now claim...

To recap, the important steps are...

Want to improve your (subject) performance in days, instead of...

What most people do when they discover something new is... But...

What you've just discovered is...

When in doubt, simply...

When you get right down to it...

Where you are at the moment (in relation to the topic) doesn't matter. What matters is...

Would any of these ideas help you to...?

Would any of these tips...

Would you like to (save, earn, profit, generate) even more...

You've read about it. Now you can do something about...

You now know how to...

Bonus Section

Keywords Into Titles

Sample Keyword Terms

write articles

write article

article writing

writing articles

how to write an article

how to write article

write research article

write newspaper article

write article summary

writing a article

how to write an article

how to write articles

write an article

write magazine article

write article review

write news article

writing an article

write online article

article re write

how to write good article

write scientific article

how to write a good article

writing a good article

write a new article

write a article

write a good article

write a travel article

how to write an online article

good article writing

writing a short article

writing a student article

write a fashion article

writing a good news article

article writing topics

article writing help

writing article summary

tips on writing an article

how to write an academic article

how to write an articles

how to write an article for a newsletter

how to write a short article

writing the name of an article

steps to writing an article

writing about articles

writing an academic article

how to write about an article

article about writing

article writing 101

write about an article

good articles to write about

writing article summaries

writing about an article

topics to write an article

how to write an outline for an article

writing an article critique

tips for writing an article

how to write opinion article

article to write about

writing academic articles

I want to write articles

writing a news paper article

write opinion articles

how to write opinion articles

writing good articles

article writing assignment

write opinion article

write your own newspaper article

I want to write an article

writing a good newspaper article

how can I write an article

tips for writing a newspaper article

how do you write a feature article

write an article about yourself

articles to write about

how to write a newsletter article

how to write articles quickly

how to write a persuasive article

how to write an article response

writing a response to an article

write a newspaper article

questions to ask when writing an article

writing an article analysis

what steps to write a good newspaper article

how to write a news paper article

how to write article analysis

how to write an effective article

how to write an informational article

persuasive writing article

writing process article

how to write a response to an article

how to write an article analysis

how to write an interesting article

how to write an analysis of an article

article writing rubric

how to write newsletter article

tips for writing newspaper articles

how to write good articles

write an articles

article writing software

article writing service

expository writing article

writing an opinion article

how to write an article summary

how to write a scholarly article

writing a student article

newsletter article writing

online article writing

article writing services

how to write article summaries

article writing tips

how to write a featured article

writing opinion articles

writing an article summary

how to write an article

writing a travel article

how to write a fashion article

writing a legal article

article writing shop

article in writing

article writing tool

automatic article writing

custom article writing

easy article writing

writing and article

free article writing

how to write a blog article

how to write a new article

how to write a travel article

write my article

write your article

write a article summary

website article writing

writing center article

article re writing

article writing site

article writing sites

best article writing

fast article writing

article of writing

article writing system

article writing company

web article writing

articles about how to write

how to write a web article

writing process articles

article writing forum

either writing articles

writing a scholarly article

writing useful articles

Random Titles Generated From Selected Keywords Above

3 Ways To Write Articles For Fun and Profit

An Article Writing Blueprint Anyone Can Use

3 Steps To Writing Articles In Just Minutes

How To Write An Article Faster Than Ever Before

Writing a Article The Quick and Easy Way

Revealed: How To Write Articles In 3 Easy Steps

Write An Article In Minutes With This Beginner's Guide

The Truth About Writing An Article In Record Time

How To Do An Article Re Write For Best Results

5 Breakthrough Ideas For Writing A Good Article

Quick Start Secrets To Develop and Write a New Article

The Unspoken Secrets About Writing A Short Article

A Step By Step System To Write A Fashion Article

The Art of Creating Unlimited Article Writing Topics

Must-Have Article Writing Help Guide

Tips For Writing An Article From a 4000+ Article Writer

How To Write Newsletter Articles Readers Love

Article Writing Tips: 5 Things You Need To Know

The Lazy Way To Find Good Articles To Write About

The Truth About How To Write An Outline For An Article Quickly and Easily

7 Sure-Fire Tips On Writing An Article Your Readers Will Love

Ever Thought "I Want To Write Articles" But Didn't Know Where To Start?

Proven Techniques For Writing Good Articles

How Can I Write An Article When I'm Not A Writer?

Stuck For Ideas? Write An Article About Yourself

Veteran Writer Shares Secrets About How To Write Articles Quickly

How To Get The Best Interview Answers By Knowing Which Questions To Ask When Writing An Article

3 Little-Known Secrets About How To Write An Online Article

Persuasive Article Writing Secrets Exposed

How To Write An Interesting Article Almost Automatically

How To Write A Good Article That Get You Traffic Effortlessly

7 Highly-Effective Online Article Writing Habits

5 Article Writing Tips Guaranteed To Double Your Productivity

Writing An Article Summary The Easy Way – Here's How

The Ultimate Article Writing Tool Anyone Can Use

Easy Article Writing Methods That Work Exceptionally Well

How To Write A New Article A Day On Autopilot

Web Article Writing For Traffic Generation

An Article Re-Write Made Easy

3 Of The Best Article Writing Tips For Increasing Productivity

An Article Writing System That Never Fails

How To Write A Travel Article The Fun, Fast and Easy Way

5 Ways Writing Useful Articles Helps Build Your Business

Above is just an example of how to get started with this process.

I used Google's Keyword Tool to build a short list of keywords related to article writing. Then I copied and pasted this list in the column on the left. To get started, I then referred to my Article Topic Idea-Starter and plugged in whatever seemed to fit. For example, I took the keyword term "write articles" and added "for fun and profit" on the end and "3 ways to" at the beginning.

See how easy this is?

There's really nothing to it. Just add whatever comes to mind and seems to make an interesting title. Use the idea-starters as they're intended. If it fits, plug it in. If something else makes more sense, use that instead. Adapt and modify. Do it quickly and you'll be off to your first (or next) batch of niche market articles in just minutes.

Start by collecting your keywords. Any number will do. But be careful not to overwhelm yourself with a massive list of thousands of keywords. The important thing is to put this process into practice.

After you've done it a few times and created your own quantity of articles quickly you can do it again. You can refine the process and customize it to your own style and preferences. You'll discover how many articles you prefer to work with at any given time as well as the number of keywords.

As you can see, doing this simple exercise generated 43 potential article titles. I could choose to go back over the list and turn virtually every term into a title. But at this point, I just wanted to get some articles written, so I'll work with I already have.

With my titles selected, all I need to do is list a few content ideas for each. This is the outlining stage where I flesh out each article by listing 3 important points that relate to the title.

So let's take a look at a few examples:

Title: 3 Ways To Write Articles For Fun and Profit

Method #1: Make a List

Method #2: Share a Personal Experience

Method #3: Teach a Mini-Lesson

Title: An Article Writing Blueprint Anyone Can Use

1. Choose Your Niche

2. Gather Niche Keywords and Prioritize

3. Transform Keywords into Titles

4. Write an Introduction

5. Provide 3 Paragraphs of Content

6. Add a Conclusion

Title: 3 Steps To Writing Articles In Just Minutes

Step #1: Let The Title Be Your Guide

Step #2: Create a Simple Map or Outline

Step #3: Use Templates To Simplify The Process

Title: How To Write An Article Faster Than Ever

Point #1: Plan It Out In Advance

Point #2: Do Your Thinking At The Planning Stage

Point #3: Use A Timer To Force Yourself To Write It Fast

I just started at the top of my titles list and worked my way down the list. You may have noticed some similarity in the titles and in fact, the list of keywords. That's par for the course in any niche. Just map out the details in each case a little differently and you'll be creating unique content as you go. The trick is to map it out rapidly.

Don't get into a mental debate about what you should or shouldn't include. Use your title as direction and capture the essential ideas.

Once you've got your content ideas listed for a number of articles, it's time to start writing. To save time, use the templates and idea-starters wherever possible. This means that launching into the writing phase is something you can do at any time. Don't wait for inspiration - just get moving. Begin by copying and pasting your article outline to a blank page. Then fill in the missing pieces.

1. Start by listing your article title.

2. Plug in an introduction template that serves your purpose and complete a paragraph.

3. Next, add at least 3 paragraphs of content by expanding upon each of the ideas presented in your outline or map.

4. Then refer to your conclusion templates to create an effective close quickly and easily.

5. Create a resource box that attracts prospects to your site. Copy and paste this to every article posted in a directory. Adjust your resource box to include your main keyword term for that article and make those words a live link back to your site.

Here's a sample article using the first example above:

3 Ways To Write Articles For Fun and Profit

Articles can make or break your online business. Most top marketers use articles on a regular basis to constantly attract as steady stream of fresh, new prospects. Articles represent content and as such, are a way to pre-sell any product, service or business.

Everyone online should write articles to build their businesses and grow their incomes. But there's one huge stumbling block that stands in the way and that is -- how can you make profitable article writing a fun and productive exercise?

Let me share three simple techniques on how to write articles for fun and profit:

Method #1: Make a List. If you can write a grocery list, you can use this simple technique to create a helpful, informative article in minutes. Just take the topic you're writing about and provide a method and sequence.

For example, if your article was about "writing articles", you would simply list the steps involved. Use numbers or bullet points to separate each step in the system.

1. Create a list of keywords.

2. Use Title Templates to turn those keywords into titles.

3. List 3 important details you want to share about the subject.

4. Write it up in sentences and paragraphs.

5. Add an introduction and conclusion.

6. Merge your resource box with your article.

To fill out your article, write a sentence or two about each point. That's all there is to creating the largest chunk of your article, the body copy.

Method #2: Share a Personal Experience. This method is effective because you're telling it like nobody else can. It's your personal experience and perspective that makes your article unique.

To write articles like no one else, share an experience through your own eyes. Deliver the information you uncovered by actually going through the experience. Start at the beginning and cover each of the important elements. This is what separates your information from theory. Your experience provides proof. When you tell your personal story, your content is sure to be 100% original.

Method #3: Teach a Mini-Lesson. Imagine that you're at the front of the room and you're teaching 20 adults enrolled in a continuing education program. The subject of your class is the subject of your article.

How can you teach someone else what you know in a way that they're sure to understand? Start with an overview of the subject. Then think back to the best teacher you ever had and recall what made them a personal favourite. Next, pretend that you're this special teacher and communicate your information in a way that makes sense.

But remember, you've only got a minute or two to cover the topic. So you need to follow your plan or overview to stay on course. Knock off one point at a time and illustrate it in a way your class will quickly grasp.

There you have it - 3 easy ways to write articles for fun and profit. Choose any method that resonates with you. One format will work best for certain topics and another format will fit others better.

But never let the task of article writing intimidate you. Make it fun and fast. Get it done and the profits will come. It isn't magic. But it can work exceptionally well for those who use these methods consistently.

Resource Box Swipe File

Learn 5 Facts You MUST Understand If You Are Ever Going to Lose Your Belly Fat and Get Six Pack Abs - http://www.sexyabsrevealed.com

Steve Manning is a master writer showing thousands of people how they can write their book faster than they ever thought possible. Here's your free book-writing library and mini-course, http://www.WriteABookNow.com/main.html

You can make money blogging. Discover how with pro blogger and copywriter Angela Booth. She'll teach you how to blog the right way, so your blog is profitable from the start, with her bestseller, "Blogging for Dollars" at http://www.abmagic.com/Blog/blogging.html

Angela's blogging ebook package has a companion blog, the Blogging for Dollars Blog at http://www.dollars2blog.com/blog/ which keeps you up to date with what's happening in the world of professional blogging.

Want to become a successful writer? Angela Booth's writing class, "Write More And Make More Money From Your Writing: Develop A Fast, Fun Productive Writing Process" at http://www.angelaswritingclasses.com/Class/writemore.html is based on lessons she developed for her private coaching students to help them to write more, improve their writing, and to make more money writing. The course trains you to become an expert writer. Her ebook "Top 70 Writing Tips To Help You To Write More" at http://www.abmagic.com/Write-More/write-more.html shows you how to end procrastination for good

Can you type? If you can type, you can create mini niche sites. Discover how easy it is to make money online with mini sites. The Mini Site Formula shows you how. Find out exactly what the Mini Site Formula can do for you at http://www.squidoo.com/best-mini-site-formula -- Go from $3 a day to $3000 a day: work from home, and work the hours you please

Discover how to make money online by writing with Angela Booth's Sell Your Writing Online NOW at http://sellwritingnow.com/Home/training.html You'll learn how to write and sell articles, blogs, ebooks and Web sites for profit, and you'll get complete training in how the Web works, so you can take advantage of the unlimited opportunities

Was your specific situation not covered in this article? You can get a free guide to Get Your Girlfriend Back that covers nearly every possible situation at http://www.getyourexbacknow.com/get_your_ex_back.htm

Want to avoid the other mines in the battlefield of love? Learn how to get your ex back and get your free guide called "Why Lovers Leave" at http://www.getyourexbacknow.com/get_your_ex_back.htm

Fortunes can be made or lost with Google Adwords. Many of the secrets to profiting with Adwords are not written in the Google guide, but you can learn them here http://www.squidoo.com/beatingadwords

If you learn better by seeing and doing, you can get "one on one" coaching for a pittance at The Wealthy Affiliate. You can get a free mini-tour of Wealthy Affiliate at http://wealthyaffiliate.wordpress.com

For a free car buying guide, inspection check off list and free search of American car auctions in your area, visit http://www.usfreeads.com/557906-cls.html -- American Car Auctions Search

Travis Sago is a computer technician and PSP enthusiast and fanatic. Don't have a good DVD ripper or video converter? You can learn more at http://www.the-psp-pimp.com/pspvideoconverter.html

Learn How to Add 11 lbs of Muscle Weight Every 7 Weeks. Build Muscle Mass Fast ==>> http://www.musclemassnow.com

Don't get confused by all the crazy fat loss myths out there. Learn 5 Facts You MUST Understand if You Are Ever Going to Lose Your Belly Fat and Get Sexy Six Pack Abs: ==>> http://www.sexyabsrevealed.com

Learn how to create your own virtual real estate empire with my free report showing you step-by-step how to create an income producing niche web business ==>> http://www.improfitreports.com

Learn how to create your own virtual real estate empire with my free report showing you step-by-step how to create an income producing niche web business using powerful article marketing ideas and cutting edge web 2.0 strategies - http://www.improfitreports.com

Grab your Free Report On: Internet Marketing Secrets That Show You Step-By-Step How to Create An Income Producing Niche Web Business Using Cutting Edge Web 2.0 Strategies - http://www.improfitreports.com

Free Report Reveals: Muscle building secrets you must know if you want to pack on massive amounts of muscle as quickly as humanly possible! - http://www.musclemassnow.com

One of the best ways to get targeted traffic to your site for free is with article marketing. I've perfected an article writing system that has literally changed people's lives and has cut their article writing time down from 1 hour per article to 7 minutes. To learn this article writing secret, go to http://www.7minutearticle.com

If you do article marketing, then you should download my report, "How to Write an Article in 7 Minutes". It shows you how to write a high quality 400-word article in 7 minutes or less, including proof reading and research. It even works on topics you know nothing about! Just go to http://www.the-article-writer.com/7minutearticle.html to get it!

By the way...do you want to learn exactly how to create a high income online business by meeting the needs of people in your niche through coaching, consulting, and teaching online classes? Download my new recording: "How to Sell High Ticket Products Online" here: http://www.highticketsellingcoach.com

---

Or...do you want to learn how to increase your online income by adding coaching, consulting, and online classes to your existing practice or business? Find out how here: Internet Marketing Coaching

---

Sean Mize teaches coaches, consultants, and small business owners how to package their knowledge and sell it in high priced coaching, consulting, and online class packages. Sean says "If you have an existing marketable service or skill that you can teach others, I can teach you to package it into a high-priced class or coaching program, guaranteed."

Do you want to learn more about how I do it? I have just completed my brand new guide to article writing success, 'Your Video Creation and Promotion Guide' -- Download it free here: Secrets of Shooting Amazing Videos Fast...

Do you want to learn how to build a big online subscriber list fast? Click here: Secrets of List Building

Sean Mize is a full time internet marketer who has written over 9034 articles in print and 14 published ebooks. Do you want to learn more about how I do it? I have just completed my brand new guide to article marketing success, 'Your Article Writing and Promotion Guide'. Download it free here: Secrets of Article Promotion

Do you want to learn how to build a big online subscriber list fast? Click here: Secrets of List Building. Sean Mize is a full time internet marketer who has written over 9034 articles in print and 14 published ebooks.

John Reese is an Internet Marketing pioneer that has been actively marketing online since 1990. John has sold millions of dollars worth of products and services online and his network of Web Sites have received over 1.4 BILLION Web Site visitors since their inception. You can learn more about John, his home study courses, and subscribe to his free newsletter by visiting: http://www.marketingsecrets.com

John Reese has been actively involved with online auctions and eBay since 1996. Mr. Reese has written several articles on the subject and has recently created the "Internet Auction Secrets" Video for teaching others how to start, run, and manage a successful online auction business from home. His 2-Hour Step-By-Step Video comes with access to a "Student's Only" web site where his students can keep up with the latest tips, tricks, and techniques. You can learn about how *you* can become one of his students at: http://www.auctionsecrets.com

NOTE to Editors: Feel free to join our affiliate program and substitute your own affiliate link for our URL in bio box. Go to http://www.auctionsecrets.com/affiliateprogram.html

NOTE2: You may run this article provided you run it with the bio box intact. Please email a copy of your publication with article in it to the author's publicist at ArticleDeptBill@rtir.com

Robert Plank, internet marketer, PHP programmer, and 23 year old homeowner, made an average of $10,000 per month every month in 2008. Check out his marketing ideas worth STEALING at: http://www.robertplank.com

Get the exact step by step formula to write a sales letter in five minutes or less, complete with easy to use worksheets and plug-n-play headlines, offers, stories, and guarantees... http://www.fiveminutecopywriting.com

Action Words Guide

Abolish	Act up
Abstract	Adapt
Accelerate	Adapted
Accelerated	Add
Accommodate	Address
Accomplish	Addressed
Accomplished	Add up
Accumulate	Add up to
Accuse	Adjust
Achieve	Adjusted
Achieved	Administer
Acquire	Administered
Acquired	Adopted
Act	Advertise
Acted	Advise
Activate	Advised
Activated	Advocate
Act like	Aid

Aide	Approve
Aided	Approved
Align	Arbitrate
Allocate	Arbitrated
Allocated	Arrange
Altered	Arranged
Amend	Arrest
Analyze	Articulate
Analyzed	Articulated
Annotated	Ascertain
Answer	Ascertained
Anticipate	Ask out
Anticipated	Assault
Applied	Assemble
Apply	Assembled
Appoint	Assess
Appointed	Assessed
Appraise	Assign
Appraised	Assigned

Assist	Back up
Assisted	Balance
Assume	Balanced
Assured	Bargain
Attain	Beat
Attained	Begin
Attend	Beg off
Attract	Bite
Audit	Blast
Audited	Block
Augment	Blow
Author	Blow up
Authored	Bolster
Authorize	Bone up on
Automate	Boost
Avert	Bought
Award	Break down
Back down	Break in (to)
Back off	Break up

Brief	Calculated
Briefed	Calibrate
Bring (take) back	Call off
Bring off	Call on
Bring up	Calm down
Broaden	Canvass
Brought	Capture
Brush up on	Care
Budget	Care for
Budgeted	Catalogue
Build	Catalogued
Build up	Catch
Built	Catch on
Bump	Catch up (with)
Burn down	Categorize
Burn up	Categorized
Butter up	Cater
Butt in	Cause
Calculate	Centralize

Chair	Clarified
Chaired	Clarify
Charge	Classified
Chart	Classify
Charted	Cleared
Chase	Climb
Check	Clip
Checked	Closed
Check in (to)	Clutch
Check off	Co-operate
Check out	Coach
Check out (of)	Coached
Cheer up	Code
Chew out	Coded
Chicken out	Collaborate
Chip in	Collaborated
Choke	Collapse
Clam up	Collar
Clap	Collate

Collect

Collected

Collide

Combine

Come across

Come down with

Come to

Comfort

Command

Commanded

Commandeer

Commence

Communicate

Communicated

Compare

Compared

Compile

Compiled

Complete

Completed

Compose

Composed

Compute

Computed

Conceive

Conceived

Conceptualize

Conceptualized

Conciliate

Conclude

Concluded

Condense

Conduct

Conducted

Confer

Confirm

Confronted

Connect

Conserve	Converted
Conserved	Convey
Consider	Conveyed
Consolidate	Convince
Consolidated	Cooperate
Construct	Coordinate
Constructed	Coordinated
Consult	Copy
Consulted	Correct
Contact	Corrected
Contacted	Correlate
Continued	Correlated
Contract	Correspond
Contracted	Corresponded
Contribute	Counsel
Control	Counselled
Controlled	Count
Convened	Count on
Convert	Crack down (on)

Cram	Dealt
Crash	Dealt with
Crawl	Debate
Create	Debug
Created	Decide
Creep	Decided
Cripple	Deck
Critique	Decrease
Critiqued	Dedicate
Cross out	Deduce
Crouch	Deduct
Cultivate	Defend
Customize	Defer
Cut	Define
Cut back (on)	Defined
Dance	Delegate
Dart	Delegated
Dash	Delineate
Deal	Deliver

Delivered

Demonstrate

Demonstrated

Depended

Depict

Depreciated

Derive

Derived

Descend

Describe

Described

Design

Designed

Detail

Detailed

Detect

Detected

Determine

Determined

Develop

Developed

Devise

Devised

Devote

Diagnose

Diagnosed

Diagram

Dictate

Differentiate

Dig

Direct

Directed

Discard

Discharge

Disclose

Discover

Discovered

Discriminate

Discuss

Dispatch

Dispatched

Dispensed

Display

Displayed

Disproved

Dissect

Dissected

Disseminate

Distinguish

Distribute

Distributed

Ditch

Dive

Diversify

Divert

Diverted

Do

Document

Dodge

Do in

Dominate

Do over

Dope

Doubled

Douse

Draft

Drafted

Drag

Drag on

Drain

Dramatize

Dramatized

Drape

Draw

Draw out

Draw up

Dress	Eat out
Drew	Edge
Drill	Edit
Drink	Edited
Drip	Educate
Drop	Educated
Drop by	Effect
Drop in (on)	Effected
Drop off	Egg on
Drop out (of)	Eject
Drove	Elect
Drown	Elevate
Drug	Elicit
Dry	Elicited
Duel	Eliminate
Dunk	Eliminated
Earn	Elope
Earned	Elude
Ease	Emerge

Empathized

Emphasize

Employ

Enable

Enabled

Enacted

Encourage

Encouraged

End up

Endure

Endured

Enforce

Enforced

Engage

Engineer

Engineered

Enhance

Enhanced

Enjoin

Enlarge

Enlighten

Enlist

Enlisted

Enrich

Ensnare

Ensure

Ensured

Enter

Entertain

Entertained

Enumerate

Equip

Erupt

Escape

Establish

Established

Estimate

Estimated

Evacuate	Expedite
Evade	Expedited
Evaluate	Expel
Evaluated	Experienced
Evict	Experiment
Examine	Experimented
Examined	Explain
Exceeded	Explained
Exchange	Explode
Execute	Explore
Executed	Explored
Exercise	Expose
Exert	Express
Exhale	Expressed
Exhibit	Extend
Exhibited	Extirpate
Exit	Extract
Expand	Extracted
Expanded	Extrapolate

Extricate	Feel
Fabricate	Feel up to
Fabricated	Fend
Face up to	Fight
Facilitate	Figured
Facilitated	Figure out
Fade	File
Fake	Filed
Fall	Fill
Fall through	Fill in
Falter	Fill in for
Familiarize	Fill out
Familiarized	Filter
Fan	Finalize
Fashion	Finalized
Fashioned	Finance
Fast	Financed
Fear	Financial
Feed	Find

Find out (about)	Flounder
Fine-tune	Flout
Finger	Flush
Fix	Fly
Fixed	Focus
Flag	Focused
Flap	Followed
Flash	Fondle
Flatten	Force
Flaunt	Forecast
Flay	Forecasted
Flee	Formalized
Flick	Formed
Flinch	Formulate
Fling	Formulated
Flip	Fornicate
Flit	Fortify
Float	Forward
Flog	Foster

Fostered	Get across
Found	Get along (with)
Founded	Get around
Frame	Get around to
Fumble	Get by
Functioned	Get in
Fund	Get off
Furnish	Get on
Further	Get out of
Gain	Get over
Gallop	Get rid of
Gather	Get up
Gathered	Give
Gauge	Give up
Gave	Gnaw
Generate	Goof off
Generated	Go out with
Gesture	Gossip
Get	Gouge

Govern	Guide
Governed	Guided
Go with	Gyrate
Grab	Hack
Grade	Hail
Graduated	Hammer
Grant	Hand in
Grapple	Handle
Grasp	Handled
Greet	Hand out
Grind	Hang
Grip	Hang up
Gripe	Harass
Grope	Haul
Grouped	Have to do with
Grow	Head
Growl	Headed
Grow up	Help
Grunt	Helped

Hesitate	Identify
Hide	Ignore
Highlight	Illustrate
Hijack	Illustrated
Hire	Imagined
Hired	Imitate
Hit	Immunized
Hitch	Impart
Hobble	Implement
Hoist	Implemented
Hold	Import
Hold up	Improve
Host	Improved
Hover	Improvise
Hug	Improvised
Hurl	Inch
Hurtle	Incorporate
Hypothesized	Incorporated
Identified	Increase

Increased	Inspected
Index	Inspire
Indict	Inspired
Individualize	Install
Induce	Installed
Induced	Instigate
Inflict	Institute
Influence	Instituted
Influenced	Instruct
Inform	Instructed
Informed	Insure
Initiate	Insured
Initiated	Integrate
Inject	Integrated
Injure	Intensified
Innovate	Interact
Innovated	Interface
Insert	Interpret
Inspect	Interpreted

Intervene	Jeer
Interview	Jerk
Interviewed	Jimmy
Introduce	Jingle
Introduced	Join
Invade	Jolt
Invent	Judge
Invented	Judged
Inventoried	Jump
Inventory	Jump all over
Investigate	Justified
Investigated	Justify
Involve	Keel
Iron out	Keep on
Isolate	Kept
Jab	Kick
Jack up	Kick out
Jam	Kidnap
Jar	Kill

Kneel	Let down
Knife	Let up
Knock oneself out	Level
Knock out	License
Label	Licensed
Lash	Lick
Launch	Lifted
Launched	Lighten
Lay off	Limp
Lead	Liquidate
Lean	List
Leap	Listed
Learn	Listen
Learned	Listened
Leave out	Litigate
Lecture	Loaded
Lectured	Lobby
Led	Localize
Left	Locate

Located	Make
Log	Make for
Logged	Make fun of
Look back on	Make out
Look down on	Make up
Look forward to	Make up (with)
Look in on	Manage
Look into	Managed
Look like	Mangle
Look over	Manipulate
Look up	Manipulated
Look up to	Manufacture
Luck out	Manufactured
Lunge	Map
Lurch	Mapped
Made	March
Maim	Mark
Maintain	Mark down
Maintained	Market

Marketed	Mimic
Mark up	Mingle
Massage	Minimize
Master	Mix up
Mastered	Mobilize
Maul	Mock
Maximize	Model
Measure	Modeled
Measured	Moderate
Mechanize	Moderated
Meddle	Modernize
Mediate	Modified
Mediated	Modify
Meet	Molded
Memorized	Molest
Mentor	Monitor
Mentored	Monitored
Merge	Motivate
Methodize	Motivated

Mourn	Nominated
Move	Normalized
Mumble	Noted
Murder	Notify
Muster	Nurse
Mutilate	Nurture
Nab	Observe
Nag	Observed
Nail	Obtain
Named	Obtained
Narrate	Occupy
Navigate	Offer
Navigated	Offered
Needle	Officiate
Negotiate	Officiated
Negotiated	Offset
Nick	Operate
Nip	Operated
Nod off	Orchestrate

Order	Page
Ordered	Painted
Organize	Pander
Organized	Panic
Orient	Pan out
Orientate	Parachute
Oriented	Parade
Originate	Paralyze
Originated	Park
Outline	Parry
Outlined	Participate
Overcame	Participated
Overhaul	Party
Overhauled	Pass
Oversaw	Pass away
Oversee	Pass out
Pack	Pat
Package	Patrol
Paddle	Pause

Paw	Pile
Peel	Pilot
Peep	Piloted
Penetrate	Pin
Perceive	Pinch
Perceived	Pinpointed
Perfect	Pioneer
Perfected	Pioneered
Perform	Pirate
Performed	Pitch
Persuade	Pitch in
Persuaded	Placate
Photograph	Placed
Photographed	Plan
Pick	Planned
Picket	Planted
Pick on	Play
Pick out	Played
Pick up	Plod

Plunge	Presented
Pocket	Preserve
Poke	Preside
Polish	Presided
Pore	Prevent
Pose	Primp
Pounce	Print
Pout	Printed
Practice	Prioritize
Praised	Prioritized
Pray	Probe
Predict	Process
Predicted	Processed
Preen	Procured
Prepare	Prod
Prepared	Produce
Prescribe	Produced
Prescribed	Professed
Present	Program

Programmed	Publicize
Progressed	Publicized
Project	Publish
Projected	Published
Promote	Pull
Promoted	Pull off
Prompt	Pull over
Proof-read	Pummel
Proofread	Pump
Propel	Punch
Propose	Purchase
Proposed	Purchased
Protect	Pursue
Protected	Push
Proved	Put away
Provide	Put back
Provided	Put off
Provoke	Put on
Pry	Put out

Put up	Rape
Put up with	Rate
Qualified	Rated
Qualify y	Rattle
Quantify y	Ravage
Question	Rave
Questioned	Read
Quit	Realigned
Quote	Realize
Race	Realized
Raid	Reason
Raise	Reasoned
Raised	Recall
Rally	Receive
Ram	Received
Ran	Recline
Rank	Recognize
Ranked	Recognized
Ransack	Recommend

Recommended

Reconcile

Reconciled

Record

Recorded

Recoup

Recreate

Recruit

Recruited

Rectify

Redeem

Reduce

Reduced

Reel

Re-evaluated

Refer

Referred

Refine

Refined

Regain

Register

Regulate

Regulated

Rehabilitate

Rehabilitated

Reinforce

Reinforced

Rejected

Rejoin

Relate

Related

Relax

Release

Relent

Remodel

Remodelled

Render

Rendered

Renegotiated	Resolve
Renew	Resolved
Reorganize	Respond
Reorganized	Responded
Repair	Restore
Repaired	Restored
Repel	Restrict
Replace	Restructured
Report	Retain
Reported	Retained
Represent	Retreat
Represented	Retrieve
Reproduced	Retrieved
Repulse	Reunited
Research	Revamp
Researched	Reveal
Reserve	Review
Resign	Reviewed
Resist	Revise

Revised	Sap
Revitalize	Satisfied
Rewrote	Save
Ride	Saw
Rip	Scale
Rip off	Scamper
Rise	Scan
Risk	Scare
Risked	Scatter
Rob	Scavenge
Rock	Schedule
Round off	Scheduled
Route	Scold
Routed	Scoop
Run into	Score
Run out of	Scout
Sail	Scrape
Salute	Scrawl
Sample	Scream

Screen	Sense
Screened	Sensed
Screw	Separated
Script	Serve
Scrub	Served
Scrutinize	Service
Sculpt	Serviced
Scuttle	Set
Seal	Set back
Search	Set goals
Searched	Settle
Secure	Set up
Secured	Sever
Seduce	Sew
Segment	Sewed
Seize	Shake
Select	Shape
Selected	Shaped
Sell	Share

Shared	Sigh
Sharpen	Signal
Shave	Simplified
Shear	Simplify
Shell	Simulate
Shield	Sip
Shift	Sit
Shiver	Size
Shock	Sketch
Shoot	Sketched
Shout	Skid
Shove	Skim
Shovel	Skip
Show	Skirt
Showed	Slacken
Show up	Slam
Shun	Slap
Shut	Slash
Sidestep	Slay

Slide	Soil
Slip up	Sold
Slug	Sold
Smack	Solicit
Smear	Solicited
Smell	Solve
Smuggle	Solved
Snap	Sort
Snare	Sorted
Snarl	Speak
Snatch	Spear
Snicker	Spearhead
Sniff	Specialize
Snoop	Specified
Snub	Specify
Snuff	Spell
Snuggle	Spike
Soak	Spin
Sock	Splice

Split	Start
Spoke	Startle
Spot	Steal
Spray	Steer
Spread	Step
Spring	Stick
Sprint	Stifle
Spurn	Stimulate
Spy	Stimulated
Squeak	Stomp
Stack	Stop
Stage	Straighten
Stagger	Strangle
Stamp	Strap
Stand	Strategize
Standardize	Streamline
Stand for	Streamlined
Stand out	Strengthen
Stand up	Strengthened

Strike	Suggest
Strip	Suggested
Stroke	Summarize
Struck	Summarized
Structure	Summon
Structured	Supervise
Stub	Supervised
Studied	Supplied
Study	Supply
Stuff	Support
Stumble	Supported
Stun	Surpass
Subdue	Surrender
Submerge	Survey
Submit	Surveyed
Substantiate	Suspend
Substitute	Sustain
Succeeded	Swagger
Suck	Swallow

Swap	Tail
Sway	Take
Swear	Take / bring back
Swerve	Take after
Swim	Take care of
Swing	Take off
Swipe	Take up
Switch	Talked
Symbolize	Tap
Symbolized	Target
Synergized	Targeted
Synthesize	Taste
Synthesized	Taught
Systematize	Taunt
Systematized	Teach
Systemize	Tear
Tabulate	Tease
Tabulated	Telephone
Tackle	Tell someone off

Tend	Tip
Tended	Toss
Terminate	Touch
Terrorize	Tour
Test	Tout
Tested	Trace
Theorize	Track
Thrash	Trade
Thread	Train
Threaten	Trained
Throw	Transcribe
Throw away	Transcribed
Throw out	Transfer
Throw up	Transferred
Tickle	Transform
Tick off	Transformed
Tie	Translate
Tilt	Translated
Time	Transmit

Transport	Tumble
Transpose	Turn
Trap	Turn around
Travel	Turn down
Traveled	Turn in
Tread	Turn off
Treat	Turn on
Treated	Turn up
Trip	Tutor
Triple	Tutored
Trot	Twist
Troubleshot	Type
Trounce	Typed
Try	Uncover
Try on	Understand
Try out	Undertake
Try out (for)	Undertook
Tuck	Undo
Tug	Undress

Unfold	Utilized
Unified	Vacate
Unify	Validate
Unite	Value
United	Vanish
Untangle	Vault
Unveil	Vent
Unwind	Verbalized
Update	Verified
Updated	Verify
Upgrade	View
Upgraded	Violate
Upheld	Visit
Uphold	Visualize
Use	Vitalize
Used	Volunteer
Usher	Wade
Utilize	Wait on
Utilize	Wake up

Walk	Win
Wander	Wired
Ward	Withdraw
Warned	Witness
Washed	Won
Watch	Work
Watch out for	Worked
Wave	Work out
Wear out	Wrap up
Wedge	Wrench
Weed	Wrestle
Weigh	Write
Weighed	Write down
Whack	Write up
Whip	Wrote
Whistle	Yank
Widen	Yell
Wield	Yield
Wiggle	Zap

Zip

Zonk out

Thank you for reading! If the information in this book was useful to you, please help us spread the word by posting your honest review on Amazon. Not only will you help the author and publisher, but you'll also help your fellow reader to make a decision. Your feedback is graciously accepted - and greatly appreciated.

Made in the USA
Lexington, KY
26 March 2014